Praise for *The S(*

'Solitaire Townsend's passion for finding answers is as infectious as it is compelling. Her core argument is brilliantly argued: move over pessimists and naysayers; the future belongs to the Solutionists.' PAUL POLMAN, AUTHOR, CAMPAIGNER AND FORMER CEO, UNILEVER

'*The Solutionists* is unusual among books on solving the world's challenges: it's easy to read, fun and optimistic. More importantly, it's an invitation to join the game of fixing the world.' ANDREW WINSTON, SUSTAINABILITY STRATEGIST AND AUTHOR OF *NET POSITIVE*

'Solitaire Townsend's unique perspective on the challenges we face enables understanding of how we can be involved in making urgent and necessary changes to the way we think about how live and work.' BARONESS YOUNG OF HORNSEY OBE

'It's rare that I finish a book by thinking that everyone who cares about the future needs to read this. But I did this time. Solitaire Townsend, a gifted storyteller, has captured the essence of what it takes to tackle the seemingly impossibly broken parts of our world and to fix them with passion, impact and joy.' JOEL MAKOWER, CHAIRMAN AND CO-FOUNDER, GREENBIZ GROUP

'Insights gained from the experts in *The Solutionists* will provide readers with fresh perspectives that hopefully spark even more innovative actions to help the planet.' TONI PETERSSON, CEO, OATLY

'This is a must-read book and call to action for sustainable and solutions focused business innovation. Solutionists can lead us to a greener, more equitable and climate-optimism-fuelled future, and this is the guide to get us there.' LEAH THOMAS, AUTHOR OF *THE INTERSECTIONAL ENVIRONMENTALIST*

'For anyone beginning to despair that all is lost, this book comes as a wake-up call that solutions are not only desperately needed but are great business opportunities, and you might have some fun along the way. It serves not just as a call-to-arms, but also as a how-to guide for anyone who's got a solution that needs unleashing on the world.' HELEN CLARKSON, CEO, CLIMATE GROUP

'Provides experience-based insights and concrete examples and guidance to help young business people become agents for change within their organizations.' TENSIE WHELAN, DIRECTOR, NYU STERN CENTER FOR SUSTAINABLE BUSINESS

'*The Solutionists* is a good reminder that each of us is the solution. It is a breath of pragmatic optimism and inspiration. Best of all, Solitaire Townsend extends an open invitation to be a part of the greatest opportunity our generation has ever had: to tackle climate change together.' VAITEA COWAN, CO-FOUNDER, ENAPTER

'We don't need another hero, we need a world of solutionists.' JON KHOO, HEAD OF SUSTAINABILITY (EAAA), INTERFACE

'This book should become a much-used reference in every business leader and changemaker's library. Solitaire Townsend's brilliant, uplifting prose reminds us that we can still rise and solve our existential challenges within our generation.' KARIMAH HUDDA, FOUNDER AND CHIEF CATALYST, ILLUMINE.EARTH

'Solitaire Townsend lifts the weight of the many challenges we face with a new way of thinking about how we build a fairer and more sustainable world. This is the book – and the motivation – we need to build the world that we can all thrive in and be proud of.' ARON CRAMER, CEO, BUSINESS FOR SOCIAL RESPONSIBILITY

'Courage and stamina are always essential, but so is the playfulness to think around corners. How joyous to find Solitaire Townsend's irrepressible energy and creativity between the covers of this book.' JOHN ELKINGTON, FOUNDER AND CHIEF POLLINATOR, VOLANS, AND AUTHOR OF GREEN SWANS

'If you enjoy saying things like "1.5°C is out of reach, we might as well prepare for the apocalypse", beware reading this book; it might just encourage you to dare to hope. If you've already taken the first courageous step of daring to imagine a better world, you'll have fun and take practical inspiration from every page!' NIGEL TOPPING, UN HIGH-LEVEL CLIMATE ACTION CHAMPION, COP26

'We have a new name for those leading change for a better world – Solutionists. Solitaire Townsend has set out clear guidance, tactics and advice for the millions more Solutionists we need.' ERIK SOLHEIM, GREEN POLITICIAN, DIPLOMAT AND SIXTH EXECUTIVE DIRECTOR, UN ENVIRONMENT

'Solitaire Townsend assembles a cast of Solutionists who combine vision, grit, flex, fun and soul to reimagine what it means to lead. Through their stories and her personal reflections, an inspiring blueprint for how to change the world takes shape.' AMANDA GARDINER, SUSTAINABILITY INNOVATION AND ENGAGEMENT HEAD, META

The Solutionists

How businesses can fix the future

Solitaire Townsend

KoganPage

First published in Great Britain and the United States in 2023 by Kogan Page Limited

2nd Floor, 45 Gee Street	8 W 38th Street, Suite 902	4737/23 Ansari Road
London	New York, NY 10018	Daryaganj
EC1V 3RS	USA	New Delhi 110002
United Kingdom		India

www.koganpage.com

Kogan Page books are printed on paper from sustainable forests.

ISBNs

Hardback 978 1 3986 0934 1
Paperback 978 1 3986 0932 7
Ebook 978 1 3986 0933 4

British Library Cataloguing-in-Publication Data
A CIP record for this book is available from the British Library.

Library of Congress Control Number
2022062093

Typeset by Integra Software Services, Pondicherry
Print production managed by Jellyfish
Printed and bound by CPI Group (UK) Ltd, Croydon, CR0 4YY

To Futerra, the best bunch of Solutionists I know.

Contents

Acknowledgements

I am immensely grateful to everyone who gifted their time and insight to me in the form of interviews and surveys – this book is about you! Special gratitude goes to Becca Warner for all of her help, and to Sarah Penrhyn-Jones and Mapem Lanigan of Futerra for filling in so many gaps. To Geraldine Collard for first commissioning this book and Matt James of Kogan Page for invaluable support as editor. Thank you to the entire Kogan Page team.

Many wonderful people helped me find and reach the interviewees in this book: Briar Goldberg, Corey Hajim and Nehemiah Rolle of TED, Tricia Thompson, Taylor Patterson and Rosie Fenning of The Earthshot Prize, Harriet Lamb and Fiona Duggan at Ashden, Laurie Lee of CARE International, Carolina Garcia Arbelaez of the 100+ Accelerator, Stephanie Klotz at Climate KIC, Jesus Chavez of Singularity Media and Cailin Wyatt, Alex Reid and Katie Rupp at Gates Ventures.

Chris Coulter of GlobeScan, Mark Lee of ERM's SustainAbility Institute and David Grayson of the Cranfield School of Management co-led the survey from which I've quoted in this book and offered their friendship throughout. Immense gratitude to the Arctic Foxes for unfailing wisdom, joy and cheerleading. To Lucy Shea, Karen Brennan, Matt Sexton and all Futerrans for so many ideas in this book. And of course, to my lovely family for unfailing love and support at every step (plus reminders to stop, rest and follow my own advice). Finally, thank you to the millions of Solutionists everywhere, who inspire me every day.

Introduction

Solutionist – noun
so·lu·tion·ist | \ -sh(ə)nəst \
Definition of Solutionist: a solver of problems

Solutionists are curious – in both meanings of that word. They are curious about the world around them, often on a lifelong quest to discover new things and find new answers. They are also curious people in that they are somewhat... odd.

I mean that in the most complimentary way, not least because I count myself among the ranks of the Solutionists. Nevertheless, I admit that being the sort of person who likes untangling knots, who is kept awake by unsolved problems and who has a strong sense that they absolutely can do something about world problems – isn't a common attitude.

It must become one. Our communities, economies, businesses and our families face an unprecedented convergence of seemingly intractable social, humanitarian and environmental crises, the most complex and daunting of which is climate change. We're all being asked questions about the future of humanity that desperately need answering.

That's a job for Solutionists. And if you're not one already, you will be by the end of this book.

For more than a quarter of a century, I've worked alongside people who are dubbed 'changemakers', 'social entrepreneurs', 'pioneers', 'creative disruptors' and, quite frequently, 'CEO'. While collaborating with, interviewing and surveying these Solutionists, I've learnt what makes them tick. I assure you, you can join these future-fixers, and if you're already leading positive change, I can help amplify your effectiveness.

The people you'll meet in this book don't tend to have many regrets, they're immensely fond of failure and, despite having compelling and remarkable visions of the future, they often value their get-things-done skills the most. They are so adaptable to circumstances that their leadership style can seem fluid, but they are so intensely attached to their values that many have held them unchanged since early childhood.

From the CEOs of global businesses like IKEA, Kao Corp and Grupo Bimbo and the chief sustainability officers of Google, AB Inbev and more, to leaders of disrupter brands like Oatly and Who Gives A Crap, plus start-up entrepreneurs in ice-batteries and insect protein, many Solutionists you'll meet in this book are wildly successful in business, founding and leading some of the most highly regarded and disruptive brands. They're transforming multinationals in ways thought impossible, inventing solutions to knotty problems and forging a new type of solutions-entrepreneurship that the world desperately needs. At least one of them has already changed the world in ways so complete that we can't remember life before his breakthroughs, and he's in the process of doing it again. Others I've met will undoubtedly do the same.

Yet they all wear it lightly, openly sharing their secrets of success and their glorious failures with me. Thousands of successful Solutionists have gifted their stories, wisdom and tools to this book. Yet almost all were surprised to be asked.

Mads Nipper, CEO of the world's largest renewables corporation, Ørsted, told me that he didn't want to take 'the credit for something I shouldn't'. Entrepreneur, model and author Lily Cole downplayed her impact, 'I'm only 34 so I feel like hopefully the best is yet to come.' Even Bill Gates told me that it's taken a 'decades-long learning process' for him to appreciate the implications of climate change.

They all were surprised to be asked about themselves, rather than their solution. I wanted to know how these folks face challenges and what wisdom they might be prepared to share – to discover the person behind the purpose. I'm rather immodestly pleased by how many of them enjoyed being dubbed 'Solutionist' as a term. It's almost as if this new wave of changemakers have been waiting for a collective noun.

Personally, I chose the job title 'Chief Solutionist' for myself during one of the long lockdowns of the pandemic.

It wasn't a familiar word, yet it perfectly encapsulated the challenge I have set myself – to focus on 'answers only' rather than wallow in my angst about the problems. For years before that, my title was 'co-founder' of Futerra, one of the world's largest and longest-established sustainability change agencies. For over 21 years we've advised clients including Unilever, Netflix, Formula 1, WWF, Gap, the United Nations and many of the businesses you'll meet in this book, both on the 'logic' of sustainability strategy and the 'magic' of purpose marketing. I love my work, but that co-founder job title only described what I did on a single day, decades ago, when I signed the papers incorporating the business. I wanted a term that describes what I do today and what I need to do tomorrow.

I claim no ownership over the word Solutionist, and I hope that in the years to come, when I search online for 'solutionist', thousands of people with that job title will pop up.

If you do decide to take on this mantle, it will likely be for one of two reasons.

First, the term Solutionist acknowledges that things need fixing. Solutionists are only required if there's a problem to solve. Does anyone think our systems and societies don't have huge challenges right now? Solutionists have rarely been more needed.

Many of the people you'll meet in this book are successful in business not despite their awareness of the devastating risk of climate change, but because of it. They don't approach social or eco-entrepreneurism and sustainable business as the latest fad or an additional value-add for business. Their companies, inventions, strategies and solutions are designed explicitly to confront problems – that's the Solutionist way.

Second, you probably like the term because you find solutions fascinating and, frankly, thrilling. Inventions, lateral thinking, creativity, unexpected answers, unusual allies and inspired business models make Solutionists literally bounce forward in their chairs.

In a survey of Solutionists, the primary benefit of working to make a difference in the world was 'sense of purpose', and the unexpected runner-up was that being a Solutionist is 'intellectually stimulating'. Solutionists are huge 'answer activists'.

You've picked up this book, so you already fulfil one criterion for being a Solutionist – you're curious (perhaps in both ways). You've bought a book with an unfamiliar word on the cover. That's a good sign for the likelihood that you're able to join the ranks of these future-fixers. Or, you are already part of the shift to a Solutions Economy where business serves a better world. Perhaps you itch to start your own business, transform your current one, invent a solution or gather with like-minded, optimistic and active people who believe we won't merely save the world – but do so in creative and inspired ways. If so, welcome. I hope this book spurs your ambition.

'Problems make me itch'

I'm a cat person and always have been. Cats require minimal logistical care and can live as near-equals, which appeals to both my indolence and my respect for independence. I'm also a vegetarian for both climate and personal-taste reasons.

Which leaves me in a pickle. Because while vegetarian cat owners might not eat meat ourselves, we buy a lot of it. Cats are one of nature's very few 'obligate' carnivores, like sharks and spiders – there are certain essential amnio acids they can only acquire through eating other animals. So, every day I had to peel open a packet of meat and leave it out in my home, if I wanted my small feline to stay. Just another of those compromises, inconsistencies and uncomfortable hypocrisies we all must live with.

Except, I happen to lead a successful sustainability firm which has Mars Petcare, one of the world's largest pet-food companies, as a client. After a bit of digging around online (with my cat gallantly trying to prevent me by sitting on the keyboard), I found a solution to my quandary – insect protein. A radically lower environmental footprint, hypoallergenic, high-quality protein which I already knew my cat would love – because I'd seen her catch and chow down on houseflies enough times.

The problem had made me itch each time I made the micro-compromise of opening traditional cat-food. It itched because I love pets, but the Nobel-prize-winning scientists of the Intergovernmental Panel on Climate Change (IPCC) have calculated that pet 'pawprints' contribute to climate change. Wanting pets to be part of a sustainable future might not seem like the most acute problem for the world right now – but it itched. Friends and family were, as usual, bemusedly accepting of my burning desire to solve this one intractable challenge.

It only took a decade to launch Lovebug cat-food, during which I learnt a great deal about vision versus execution, my own limitations as a leader and the absolute sorcery a great team can accomplish. There were massive obstacles – such as securing warehouses and delivery logistics during a quarantine. And thrilling moments, like holding the first beautifully packaged bag in my hand. Lovebug's now a rapidly growing pet-food brand which feeds cats insect-only food in 100 per cent recyclable packaging. It's won awards and, thankfully, my cat Skye adores it enough to regularly attack the bag to try to gorge herself on the kibble.

That singular problem no longer itches my brain. One itchy problem down, only 500 or so more to go!

I tell this story because it demonstrates how solutions emerge from a set of attributes and attitudes which are greater than the sum of their parts. Solutions like these are an emergent property of Solutionists.

The first part of this book is dedicated to the five points of what I call the Solutionist star – the special,

FIGURE 0.1

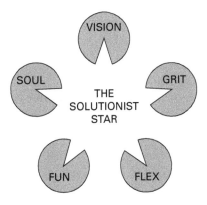

but learnable, attributes and attitudes that successful Solutionists embody (Figure 0.1). The second half will set out how to deploy your star to create transformative change.

Your star is very straightforward, yet with a great deal of depth to explore. In the simplest terms, it's made up of five points:

1 Vision – optimistic purpose, informed by the future we want.
2 Grit – hard-working hope that never gives up on the vision.
3 Flex – changing plans, failing fast and adapting as many times as needed.
4 Fun – finding the positive in the problem, building teams and enjoying the ride.
5 Soul – having a calling to make a difference in the world.

Over the next few chapters, I'll unpack the star, revealing unexpected interfaces between the points and how to balance them out. You'll discover more about yourself, and how to build teams that complement your own star's strengths and limitations. Then we'll work on what you're going to do with it. There are formulas for success, new skills to discover and traps to avoid. I'll set you one of the biggest (and most awesome) challenges of your life.

Because, together, we'll plot out how we're going to solve climate change, heal social inequity, remake our economies, grow our businesses and bend the arc of history towards justice, while enjoying every minute of it.

Did the hard slap of cynicism hit you while reading that? Don't worry, that's common when you start thinking like a Solutionist. The ghouls of fatalism, apathy and 'what-about-ism' have always stalked every attempt to find answers to the world's greatest problems. Today, they infect social media, boardrooms and even families and friends of newbie Solutionists. Probably, even your own heart harbours doubt that we can 'solve' some of our big problems, timidity about whether you're the right person and anxiety about the risk of even trying. I promise you, we may be racing against Armageddon but we can still choose an awesome adventure.

In Chapter 10 on 'joyful entrepreneurialism', I'll coach you through the natural anxiety and motivation-sucks every Solutionist faces. And in Chapter 6 on 'hope is a business plan', we'll dive into exactly what solutions will genuinely transform the world.

You'll also meet, and join, a huge movement of people who embody the adage that 'people who say it can't be done, shouldn't interrupt those who are doing it'.

Solutionists everywhere

This is a business book, written for those with an entrepreneurial spirit and a conviction that industry can be part of the solution.

These insights also apply to Solutionists in non-profit and activist roles, in governments and policy making, in education and the public sector, in indigenous cultures and community building, and in families everywhere.

If you're one of the many non-commercial Solutionists changing the world, I hope this book, especially the sections on the Solutionist star, will serve you well, not least because no part of society can function, or exist at all, without the rest. Most of the commercially minded Solutionists I interviewed took pains to emphasize how much, and how often, their business has depended upon government support, community acceptance and strong social systems. Traditionally, titans of business and famous entrepreneurs discount or omit to mention how their success depends on society or early subsidy. The mythology of the superhuman entrepreneur building their empire through sheer will and genius permeates our social discourse – from Henry Ford to Elon Musk.

The new Solutionists do embody many of those attributes – especially strong purpose, tenacity and creativity. However, because they are set on solving social and environmental problems, rather than solely building their own fortune (and ego), they acknowledge their interdependence on society and environment.

In the very next chapter, on the Solutions Economy, we'll discover why that attitude serves Solutionists so well and how the future of business will be shaped by their unusual and vitally needed approach.

A century of solutions

No dastardly villain plotted in their hilltop lair to destroy our climate. Even those blinkered souls who clung until recently to soon-obsolete fossil fuels were more ignorant than evil. Although, going forward, anyone who defends fossil fuels might have a whiff of the cackling baddie about them.

For the world's social inequities, however, the immorality has been obvious for the entire modern era. Think about the woman who grew the beans for your morning cup of coffee (or tea, cocoa, palm oil in your croissant and other commodities) and how desperately poor she probably is. She'll make hard choices about whether her child is sick enough to pay to see a doctor, or her kids are needed more on the farm than at school. Every day she'll fight to ignore the gnawing anxiety in her gut about what will happen to her family if just one more thing goes wrong. With the global pandemic hitting supply chains, many of her problems have been horribly exacerbated. The world's 500 million smallholder farmers are some of the poorest people in the world; as legendary Harvard professor Jane Nelson puts it, 'Even those farmers who are integrated into the supply chains of largest-scale agricultural enterprises… do not always earn a living income' (Nelson, 2019). And our global food system depends, for its profit margins, on keeping them that way. If nothing else, your coffee being mixed with penury should be enough to spark your Solutionist itch.

It did for Tony's Chocolonely. If you haven't tried their delicious chocolate, I recommend you do (my favourite is the salted caramel). Instead of a chocolate bar's typical neat rows of squares, these bars have uneven, irregularly shaped chunks to represent the continued income inequalities and slavery in the cocoa industry. In 2020, over 1.5 million children still worked illegally in the cocoa supply chain in Ghana and Ivory Coast alone (NORC, 2020), as well as 30,000 victims of modern-day slavery (Walk Free Foundation, 2018). Tony's Chocolonely (which now has 20 per cent of the chocolate market in the Netherlands and is sold in over 20 countries (Brown, 2019)) guarantees your sweet tooth will be guilt free, at least in terms of zero slavery in their supply chain. Their plan is simple, as Henk Jan Beltman, CEO of Tony's Chocolonely told me:

> First, there is a problem, we need to solve it. Second, we must set a clear example to make sure that it works, not only on the sustainable side, but also on the business side. So, we will grow faster, make more profit, have better numbers, deliver a stronger brand than any other chocolate maker out there. Third, we must open up so that other people can join, because only together can we make this work.

This is a pure Solutionist approach, and we need so much more of it. Climate change and poverty are the two giant monsters that Solutionists must walk towards, fist balled and weapons raised. They are also emblematic of a multitude of other interconnected and intersectional issues – biodiversity loss, gender inequality, water scarcity, social injustice, plastic pollution, hunger crisis, soaring inequality, global conflict and an ever-expanding list of unfair and dangerous trends that have been left unchecked for too long.

I state all this outright, here in the introduction to this book, not to depress or overwhelm you. Instead, because we are right on the cusp of shifting from standing frozen in the headlights of these horrors to digging our heels in, refusing to budge and stopping them.

As Henk Jan, the chocolate CEO, went on to say, 'I'm fucking stubborn. You need to realize if it doesn't work the first, the second or the third time, it doesn't mean it cannot work. And if you stand up one more time than you fall down, you're successful.'

We'll need that stubbornness. We're just over two decades into what I call the 'solutions century', an era in which we'll accept the benefits that industrialization has gifted us and unflinchingly face and fix the harms that progress unleashed. In doing so we'll kickstart a solutions revolution that will propel human wellbeing, equity and experience to a future worth living in. It's worth mentioning, as an entrepreneur myself, that this transformation will also be worth trillions of dollars.

I'm immensely grateful to every Solutionist I've interviewed for this book, those who have filled in surveys and those whose work I've referenced. Not everyone I have profiled in this book agrees with each other on the answers. Solutionists are fiercely independent and often better at accepting consequences than compromises. Trying to capture the essence, strategies and collective wisdom of such a wildly diverse set of people and perspectives hasn't been easy. Decades into my own service to existing solutions and search for new ones, I'm immensely grateful for the chance to try.

I chose a star to represent Solutionists because stars symbolize direction and guidance. Throughout history, mariners have charted a course by them, when all other landmarks and certainty are lost. Today, we need that positive light more than we ever have, as humanity charts our own course towards a Solutions Economy. As Bill Gates told me, 'I'm an optimist who tries to be realistic. We can get to net-zero emissions, but it will be the hardest thing people have ever done.'

Are you up for the challenge?

CHAPTER ONE

Welcome to the Solutions Economy

Over the past few months, I've bumped into a 6-foot-tall, walking, roaring, dinosaur called Frankie in the corridors of the United Nations, at the big advertising festival in Cannes and then on a TED talk stage. I jumped with surprise each time.

You might already have seen the video of Frankie giving a speech at the UN. If not, join the millions who have watched the 'Don't Choose Extinction' campaign on YouTube. Frankie has a simple message, 'Imagine if we had spent hundreds of billions per year subsidizing giant meteors! That's what you're doing right now!' (UNDP, 2021).

Frankie is spokes-dinosaur for a UN campaign to challenge fossil-fuel subsidies, and a wildly creative way to make such an esoteric issue interesting. Although, the current situation should be infuriating even without Frankie nudging us to avoid his fate.

In 2022, IPCC scientists from every UN country agreed that existing and currently planned fossil-fuel projects (oil, coal and gas extraction) are already more than our climate can handle and could be devastating for civilization as we know it. And yet, in 2022, taxpayers around the world subsidized oil, gas and coal companies to the tune of over $5.9 trillion, according to the IMF (2022). Divided across humanity (7.8 billion people as of 2021 (World Bank, 2021)), each of us gives at least $756 of our own money to fossil-fuel companies per year.

For comparison, the extreme poverty line for a human being (adult or child) is designated at $2.15 per day, so just $785 per year (World Bank, 2022). Those fossil subsidies could wipe out extreme poverty overnight. Instead, our taxes are directly bankrolling further climate chaos.

Today's global economy is riddled with a mind-bending array of these illogical and infuriating messes. Governments spend our money building new airports instead of public transport. Investment that could go into wind farms pours into fracking. More people have access to a mobile phone than access to a proper toilet. As pressures like climate change and social division build, these cracks are starting to show in our economies and in the societies they are supposed to support.

Of course, climate change is also the endgame for the old economy, because in any competition of finance versus physics, physics always wins.

Young people are especially sensitive to this fracturing system. In millions of social media posts, they darkly joke about #latecapitalism and them being the #lastgeneration on earth. According to research that my firm Futerra conducted with Ipsos MORI, as many as one in five young people now believe it is 'too late to fix climate change'. Without hope, it's hard to feel motivated enough to imagine and create solutions. Start-ups and science labs, boardrooms and public offices – all need young, inspired thinkers and doers. Unfortunately, when polled by Gallup, a whopping 85 per cent of people are unhappy at work and many worry they are in what anthropologist David Graeber termed 'bullshit jobs' – work that provides no real utility or benefit to the world (Clifton, 2017; Graeber, 2018).

In multiple surveys across the world, most people believe capitalism in its current form is doing more harm than good.

So far, so downbeat, eh? Don't worry, I'm still Chief Solutions.

These cracks in the system are being inexorably forced from the outside by climate change, inequality, war and pandemics all rupturing an economic order never built to cope with them. But, the pressure is also mounting from the inside.

I believe another economy, more fit for the moment, is growing within the shaky edifice of the current one, forcing its way into existence. It doesn't fit the existing model's shell – it is an altogether different shape. It belongs to a new mould, one whose curves and corners have been formed by today's landscape of both mounting crises and booming creativity.

The opportunity is astonishing. Lack of certainty and shaky foundations can be unsettling; alternatively, this shiny new system is already raking in success. Too often, its bright outline is obscured in our media discourse on the rumblings, upheavals and discontents in the old system. Look closer for the signs; an explosion of entrepreneurialism, a nexus of new technology and new business models, experiments with new forms of capital and, of course, more and more Solutionists deciding to step up.

The potential gains aren't those traditionally promised to 'responsible' business. Over the past decades a neat, yet lacklustre, business case has emerged for sustainable business practice and environmental and social governance (ESG). Energy and material efficiencies can save costs, solid ESG commitments can motivate and retain staff, being more purposeful helps brands connect with consumers. Markets have learnt that good sustainability tends to mean good governance overall. Responsible businesses are a safe pair of hands.

All valid benefits, all proven over time, all rather tame. The Solutions Economy explodes those benefits into nothing less than a total market transformation, quite literally an entrepreneur's dream.

In 2022 McKinsey modelled the implications of a world in which the UN's climate goals are met, which, bluntly, we can't afford not to do. They conclude that in what I call a Solutions Economy, 'This wholesale shift toward institutions and projects that emit minimal greenhouse gases (GHGs) may create the largest reallocation of capital in history.' As they point out, financial institutions responsible for more than $130 trillion of capital have already declared that they will manage their assets in ways intended to hold warming below 1.5°C.

McKinsey goes on to prophesize that demand for climate solutions 'would trigger unprecedented capital reallocation: $3.5 trillion in new spending on low-emissions assets each year through 2050. Another $1 trillion per year that now goes toward high-emissions assets would instead pay for low-emissions capital stock' (McKinsey, 2022).

The financial win is impressive and challenges the orthodoxies of the old economy that we can't afford climate action. In the Solutions Economy, solving climate change solves everything else.

Later in this book, we'll explore the technologies, business models and sectors where the biggest upheavals are happening, so the biggest fortunes are waiting to be made. This new economy rising from the ashes of the old is the greatest entrepreneurial opportunity since the Industrial Revolution. And this time, the benefits can be grasped by everyone.

Well, everyone who gets what's going on.

Seeing the light

The economist, Harvard Business School professor and author, Rebecca Henderson, told me a story of how hard some people find grasping the speed of change:

> Many senior business people have trouble grasping how quickly the world is changing. A little while ago, I spent more than an hour trying to persuade a group of senior business people that climate change was going to upend their world.

It was uphill work. One of them – he was in the fossil fuel business – reflected that he'd spent twenty years building his company but that now 'everyone hated him'. Others wondered whether it was 'really such a big deal'. While there are CEOs who understand what's happening in a deep way – the CEOs of Chobani or Impossible Foods, for example – it can be difficult for people who have spent their entire careers maximizing profits to switch gears. The good news is that more and more businesses are being pushed by their employees and their customers to think about these issues, and as that happens, we're seeing more firms exploring self-regulation and the possibility of industry-wide co-operation as a result. But it's going to take work – and pressure! – to persuade firms to focus on doing the right thing. That group of senior business people? Things changed when I asked them what their children thought about climate change. After that there was no stopping the conversation.

Rebecca is one of the brilliant minds plotting out what a new economy might look like, and how to get there. In her groundbreaking book, *Reimagining Capitalism in a World on Fire*, she proposes how to rebalance the relationship between the market and public institutions, to correct for the 'market failures' of climate change and rampant inequality. Hers is a vision of how we can 'rewire' our systems towards more purposeful business that welcomes smart regulation as a benefit, not a curse. For Rebecca, in a Solutions Economy, the state and the market become collaborators rather than competitors. Why would business leaders choose that path? Because without that collaboration, the external pressures, especially of climate change, would crash our economies anyway. Radically reimagining capitalism is the only way to save it.

Kate Raworth, Senior Research Associate at Oxford University, takes the rethink even further in her famous concept of Doughnut Economics. She challenges the outdated obsession markets have with growth at all costs and points out that Gross Domestic Product (GDP) was created in the 1930s but is now expected to measure a 21st-century economy which is 10 times larger. GDP contains so many of those illogical aspects that make the old economy so unfit for the modern world. It ignores the value of unpaid labour like housework or caring for elders and GDP increases every time someone gets cancer – not the kind of growth most of us would welcome in the real world. Rather than a linear upward line of growth, Kate proposes a doughnut with measures of planetary health around the outside and social wellbeing on the inside. Economies should seek to stay within the yummy ring between the two – delivering the greatest quality of life for citizens without breaking planetary boundaries.

Cities like Amsterdam, Brussels, Copenhagen, Berlin and Cambridge are trialling doughnut economic measures for their citizens. And her ideas are spreading through how young economists think about their work. This type of model is central to how a Solutions Economy would function, by measuring what people actually want.

Big thinker Carlota Perez takes a lateral approach to this new economy. She doesn't want to stop or slow growth, she wants to dematerialize it. 'Green won't spread by guilt and fear, we need aspiration and desire,' she says. She sees signs we are already redefining the 'good life' and that 'smart green growth' will be fuelled by desire for new, sustainable and aspirational lifestyles (Wittenberg-Cox,

2020). The inspired economist Mariana Mazzucato is asking fundamental questions about how 'value' has been defined, who decides what that means, and who gets to measure it. 'If some people are value creators,' she asks, 'what does that make everyone else? The couch potatoes? The value extractors? The value destroyers?' She wants to make economics explicitly serve the people, rather than explain their servitude (2019).

These are just a few of my favourite visionaries. After decades of inertia in economics, and mere tinkering at the edges, we're now witnessing an explosion of new thinking and busting of old paradigms. And it's not only academic economists asking these questions. Even some of the world's largest businesses are starting to challenge the linear system and invent new models.

In 2019 people around the world made one billion visits to IKEA stores (Statista, 2022). There have been claims that more copies of its catalogue (now replaced with an eco-friendly digital version) were printed each year than the Bible or the Quran. IKEA's DIY-furniture approach has already transformed a market once. Today, they are upending their business model again. Launched in 2021, their 'buyback and resell' option now has IKEA pay their customers for no-longer-wanted furniture, which the store then goes on to resell in the 'Circular Hub' area of the shop. This has the potential to prevent more than half of the company's potential waste products from reaching landfill – and their new model has helped slash the company's carbon footprint as well as spark an uptick in sales. Paying to buy back your own products might seem counterintuitive under old economic rules, but Jesper Brodin, IKEA's CEO, was clear to me about the need for change:

> If you're in a boat that's sinking, you might run into people who deny that you're sinking; well, I wouldn't spend too much time on those people. If you believe, like I do, that this is an existentialistic time for humanity, then you have to be able to look yourself in the mirror and say, 'Maybe I'll run into some obstacles, but at least I took the responsibility to do what I felt was right.' Easy to say, but I think that's an incredibly important decision. I've met so many senior leaders who regret not taking the chance to stand up for what they thought was right. Right now, we're shaping economy 2.0. In that economy, equality and climate action are tangible benefits of the economic model. And if you're not part of that, your brand simply won't last. In that unknown lies the opportunity.

Or as Paul Polman, the legendary former CEO of Unilever put it to me, 'The business community now sees not only a fractured society, but that it's becoming a fractured world. And as I always said, business cannot succeed in these societies that fail.'

What about net zero?

You've probably heard of 'net zero', one of the dullest terms for an exciting idea I've ever heard (and sustainability isn't short of explosive ideas dressed in boring words and acronyms).

Unlikely as it sounds, reaching net zero is the catalyst for that flip towards the Solutions Economy. It's also how we make sure our kids aren't the #lastgeneration.

Net zero means cutting carbon emissions right down, then 'compensating' for the carbon you can't cut – by investing in carbon removals. So not 'absolute zero', which means emitting no carbon at all, or 'carbon neutral', where you pay to offset your emissions.

While there are different definitions of how much you need to cut before you can claim to be net zero, most experts agree you need to have reduced your carbon, against a baseline, by at least half by 2030, then by 90 per cent by 2050 (SBTi, 2021). Ideally, you'll invest in carbon removals all through that time, by helping to restore nature (e.g. soils, forests and wetlands that sequester carbon), or in technology that sucks carbon out of the air.

Ok, so even I struggled to make all that sound interesting. Essentially, we have to balance the world's climate books, which are currently in serious bankruptcy territory. More than 70 countries, including the biggest polluters – China, the United States and the European Union – have set net-zero targets, covering about 76 per cent of global emissions (UNEP, 2021).

In our interview, Bill Gates explained the urgency for all this:

> Unless we move fast toward net-zero emissions, bad things will happen well within most people's lifetime. We've already begun to see how weather patterns are changing – maximum temperatures and climate-related disasters like wildfires are much more frequent than anyone expected. Even if climate

change didn't rank as an existential threat to humanity, it will make everyone worse off, and it will make the poorest even poorer. Building climate consensus and global cooperation is the challenge. It's hard to get every country in the world to agree on anything – especially when you're asking them to incur some new cost, like the expense of curbing carbon emissions. No single country wants to pay to mitigate its emissions unless everyone else will too.

So, for him, the answer is for the economy to make the case for action within itself. He added that 'Investing in green innovation will lead to new industries and job creation.'

It's that last part of that puzzle – green innovation and new industries – where things get properly interesting. Because not one of those countries or businesses wants to reach net zero by shutting up shop, reducing quality of life or going backwards in terms of human progress. Although sometimes I wonder if that's what people think net zero means.

Instead, those massive reductions in carbon will require massive innovations, huge investments and the creation of entire new industries. As the McKinsey report puts it, 'Economic output would progressively (and permanently) tilt away from goods and services that are emissions-intensive and toward those that can be made and used without emitting GHGs… generating more than $12 trillion of annual sales by 2030' (McKinsey, 2022).

I told you this is a trillion-dollar chance to save the world.

Google is one of the businesses I work with that see this potential for the Solutions Economy. Kate Brandt, their Chief

Sustainability Officer, has overseen Google's invention of smart home thermostats which helped people cumulatively save more than 105 billion kilowatt-hours of energy – equivalent to double Portugal's annual electricity consumption. As experts in handling huge amounts of information, they now help cities time traffic lights to minimize idling, and in Google Maps the algorithm now picks eco-friendly driving routes – helping to avoid more than half a million metric tons of carbon emissions. None of this is their 'direct' responsibility; Google is managing that aspect by working towards running every data centre and building directly on renewables by 2030. They are inventing these new products because, as Google itself says on its website, climate change is 'both a complex challenge for which solutions are desperately needed and one of the greatest opportunities for innovation, creative problem solving, and collaborative action in human history' (Google, 2022).

Kate explains that thinking:

> Yes, we need companies to look at their operations and their value chains, but it must not stop there. Because the biggest business opportunities are when you go beyond that, and you actually look at the role of your core products. We can turn net zero into a strategic initiative that creates value, that's part of strategic planning, that's part of product roadmaps. When I hear companies just being very focused on, 'Okay, we've made these commitments in our operations and it's hard and it's expensive, and we're working on it,' I'm like, 'Okay, that's good. That's fabulous. Well done. And, what else? How do you think about the role of your business in the solution?'

For Google and many other companies waking up to the potential of the Solutions Economy, the choice is simple, as Kate says, 'Businesses who do this right are going to survive and thrive and see a huge long-term investment, and businesses that don't are going to become extinct.'

The only constant is change

Many industries have faced extinction before, even as they argued against their fate.

'In the present circumstances of the country, trade ought to be encouraged instead of being shut from those places which are still open to us' (Hansard, 1806). These words were written in defence of an industry which was being heavily criticized. Leaders in the industry accused critics of not having their facts straight. Many worried that ending the market would destroy the economy, arguing it should be slowly reformed. National security might be risked, and cool heads should be allowed time to plan a careful transition.

All these are the well-documented arguments made by British slave traders against abolition in the 1800s. They sound a lot like arguments made by big oil companies today. It's a deeply uncomfortable analogy, yet one that Reverend Lennox Yearwood Jr of the Hip Hop Caucus made for me during an event on climate justice. He campaigns for total divestment from fossil fuels, understanding all too well how climate events unfairly hit black and vulnerable communities first: 'Our parents fought for equality in the 20th century but in the 21st century, we're fighting for existence.'

Removing horrible injustices from our economies didn't destroy them; instead, it spurred progress. There are so many other examples, from the port city of Liverpool changing from burning millions of tonnes of whale-oil in street lamps to switching on electric light, to typing pools being replaced by word-processors. Adapting to necessary change isn't just possible, it's what drives innovation.

You will likely have experienced at least part of the world's most recent revolution: the dawn of the digital age. It has upended our lives at home and at work (who remembers life before mobile phones?), revolutionized global trade and spread ideas at a previously unimaginable pace. You've already lived through one transformation; is it so hard to imagine another?

How do we get there?

Every year, a mind-boggling 2 billion tons of waste goes to landfill – enough to fill trucks that would encircle the planet 24 times (The World Counts, 2022). We've designed too many things that simply can't be recycled. Perhaps.

For TerraCycle, landfill should never be needed. They invent ways to recycle things others can't: crisp packets and coffee capsules, plastic toys and toothpaste tubes. Households, offices, schools and other organizations can send them hard-to-recycle packaging, which TerraCycle then turn into a raw material that they sell on to companies who can use it – like manufacturers of outdoor furniture or playgrounds.

Brilliant, but they realized it's still just trying to clean up the old economy.

To cut off waste before it's made, TerraCycle invented Loop – a Solutions Economy idea in practice. Loop offers shoppers the brands and products they love, delivered to their door, in beautiful stainless-steel branded packaging which, when you're done with it, gets picked up and refilled. From shampoo to breakfast cereal, laundry detergent to peanut butter – no box, bottle, can or carton ends up as trash.

Trialled through Walmart in the United States and Tesco in the UK, Loop has now been rolled out in Canada, Australia, Japan and France, and includes 500 products from 150 companies. Tom Szaky, the founder of Loop, didn't hold back explaining to me why he turns systems like this on their head:

> What I see in business right now is that the god of profit is still a mono-deity being worshipped. Ok, profit's not an evil thing, but it should be no more than an indicator of business health. Profit is like having a good heartbeat, without a heartbeat you die, with a good heartbeat you live. But just having a heartbeat isn't worth living for – it's there so you're able to dance the dance of life. As a business we should operate in this holistic way, and the way to do that is make profit an indicator of health, not the purpose of being.

Tom is already building Solutions Economy businesses. To speed even more of them, we need to get a few things right.

1. Take back control

Markets make a terrific servant, but a terrible master and a terrifying god. Somehow we've forgotten that capitalism serves society, not the other way round. By contrast, in the Solutions Economy, businesses are judged by the impact of their solution as a ratio of the resources and labour they use.

Or, even more simply:

Resource use < positive impact = Solutions Economy

Resource use > positive impact = Old Economy

Uyunkar Domingo Peas Nampichkai is an indigenous Achuar leader from the Ecuadorian Amazon. He is Territories Coordinator for the Amazon Sacred Headwaters Initiative which is forging a partnership between the public and private sectors, under indigenous leadership, to protect vast swathes of the Amazon from exploitation. He put the options very directly to me, 'Businesses are always focused on the material world and are unsatiable, they just keep wanting more and more. They have power and resources; they should be a force for good.'

We must become insatiable for solutions.

2. Bold solutions capital

Investing in the Solutions Economy centres on long-term benefits instead of making a quick buck, and sees opportunity where others overlook it. It identifies where money can go that matters and how this can offer meaningful – often higher – returns. Fresh Coast Capital turns underused urban land into tree farms, to create climate resilience and revitalize neighbourhoods – all while increasing the land's financial value. This is solutions capital at work.

With the huge Inflation Reduction Act announced in the United States, capital for solutions has been unleashed like never before. The Act includes roughly $370 billion to address climate change in ways that will reduce risk for even more private capital to join in (US Congress, 2022). The money includes incentives to make buying an electric vehicle (EV) or investing in renewable energy both cheaper and very low risk. The plan is to make US renewable energy the cheapest in the world.

Credit Suisse reports that the Act could spur $1.7 trillion for solutions over the next decade. They conclude that for big corporations, the Inflation Reduction Act 'definitively changes the narrative from risk mitigation to opportunity capture' (Meyer, 2022).

3. Radical new business models

In Chapter 6 on 'Hope is a business plan', we'll trigger your solutions itch with all the emerging business opportunities. New business models are budding at such a rate it's hard to keep up, and these are the approaches that excite me right now:

- Circular – turning waste into an asset, repair and upcycling, product to service, leasing, resale, sharing and resource recovery. This is a huge movement dismantling the 'take–make–use–waste' linear system and releasing the value trapped within it. The wildest example of this model I could find is DYCLE. These biodegradable diapers are collected when 'full' and composted down into super-fertilizer – highly valuable for farming. Rather than building a waste mountain of plastic diapers, your baby can help grow an orchard of fruit trees.

- Equitable – employee ownership, co-operatives, fair pricing, micro-finance, community-interest companies and profit sharing. Businesses aren't destined to exploit their workforce or suppliers. You might be surprised to know that 10% of the world's employed people already work in a cooperative, where they co-own their company (International Cooperative Alliance, 2016). Could we imagine everyone having a stake in the game?
- Dematerialized – 'virtual' tourism to digital fashion; as we spend more time online, the 'stuff' we crave can come as pixels rather than products. For just $17.99 you can buy a 'virtual' pair of Gucci trainers that cost over $500 in physical form – worn in Roblox and other games. Virtual products may soon outpace physical ones in some sectors.

From the B Corp movement, where purpose is protected in governance, to tech start-ups deploying crypto to value ecosystem services, new models abound. We need millions more.

4. Play the long game

When I asked Bill Gates what business leaders need to change today, he was clear that:

> We need to invest in climate as a long-term issue. Often there is too much focus on near-term goals, like reducing emissions

by 2030. It's good that there's a level of accountability in short-term goals because, for example, policymakers could still be in office when commitment dates come up. But short-term investment in climate change tends to not focus on the hard problems, the ones with longer lead times like agriculture and industrial emissions. We won't make a big enough difference if we only focus on short-term.

5. Tell the solutions story

This one is simple. Solutions must become the story of our economy: dominating our finance media, obsessed over by venture capitalists and thoroughly unpacked, analysed and taught in every business school.

Then the new story will spark huge capital flows into innovative business models with a long-term strategy. This is how we build a Solutions Economy. How will we know when we get there? When more value is being generated by the solutions than by the problems. Or, when the curve of emissions is heading down while measures of human progress are heading up.

As the new economy rises from the ashes of the old, it's unlikely to be neat or pretty. And it doesn't need to be. The Solutions Economy isn't an environmentalist nirvana of moral capitalism (or, indeed, no capitalism at all). It will be a competition, green in tooth and claw – one in which the Solutions win by sweeping away the confused, slow-moving, excuse-laden old economy.

Many of us are already living and succeeding in the Solutions Economy. In the next few chapters, I'll show you how to join us.

EXERCISE   Solutions starters

Following each chapter in this book, you'll find a box like this. Within it I'll offer practical tips, actions and exercises to spark your Solutionist journey.

For this chapter the exercise is easy: try pitching the Solutions Economy back to yourself.

1   Imagine you're making a speech about it, explaining it to someone over dinner or talking to a young graduate about how the economy will change in their lifetime.

2   I'm a fan of pitches made up of polemic backed up by facts. You might centre your pitch around case studies of solutions, or set out a compelling story of the future. Perhaps the $130 trillion of capital due to be invested in solutions is the only pitch you need.

3   However you phrase it, put the Solutions Economy in your own words.

4   Try doing it right now, or practise your speech in the shower, think it through on the treadmill or even give it for real to colleagues and friends.

Because the more people know a Solutions Economy is possible, the sooner it will arrive.

CHAPTER TWO

Your star

When I explained the premise of this book to Jesper Brodin, the CEO of IKEA, he said, 'You know what, I thought I would write that book, but now you're doing it, so that's all good.'

I promised him I would find the elixir of changemaking – that special magic that emerges when someone marries their deep sense of purpose with the ability to actually get things done, and that I would discover how everyone could learn how to become a Solutionist.

This is what I found. I hope you approve, Jesper.

Making changemakers

As I interviewed and surveyed Solutionists, a pattern began to emerge of what makes them special. All demonstrated similar attributes and attitudes, in their own unique ways. When they spoke to me of unhelpful failures and times they didn't 'show up' in a good way, it was always because they'd neglected part of what makes them shine.

The wall of post-it notes in my study coalesced as I kept researching the leadership style of great changemakers. From Nelson Mandela to Malala Yousafzai, Rachel Carson to Dr B R Ambedkar, Helen Keller to Millicent Fawcett – I drew inspiration from the people who have shaped our world for the better.

A Post-it picture of five clear points emerged, which, when embodied by changemakers, super-charged them into Solutionists (Figure 2.1).

On the right, grit and flex are what I call attributes. In the structure proposed by psychologist and Nobel Laureate Daniel Kahneman, in *Thinking Fast and Slow*, these are both System 2 ways of thinking – slow, deliberate and requiring concentration. Some people call it 'left brain thinking'.

On the left, soul and fun are attitudes. These are more System 1 ways of being – automatic, built-in, 'right brain' thinking.

I almost hesitate to use those simple binaries of left brain/right brain or System 1 and 2. Because although grit and flex are more conscious/learnt, they can also simply become part of who you are. Plus, a social conscience and light-hearted approach to solutions can also be a deliberate choice – as we'll discover later in this chapter. I make the analogy because in my interviews it was clear that being a Solutionist is a rounded mindset and way of being, encompassing both hard choices and a deep sense of self.

FIGURE 2.1

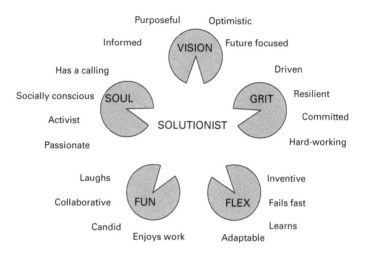

Those who enjoy symbolism will notice the image is a gestalt model, where the star is only there because each point is aligned a certain way. Without all the component parts, the star doesn't exist. Becoming a Solutionist emerges from learning, practising and embodying the five points, not by aiming for the middle.

The point of vision

Vision for Solutionists manifests in complementary ways:

- Purposeful – many of the people I interviewed quoted Mark Twain to me, 'The two most important days in life

are the day you are born, and the day you find out why.'
Every single one personified that quote, because of the
centrality of purpose in their lives. Paul Polman, former
CEO of Unilever, put it as, 'Having a strong sense of
purpose allows you to deal with a lot of these bumps
along the road, because you know that it's not an easy
journey, otherwise someone would have done it before
you already.' Jesper Brodin, CEO of IKEA, was blunt
that, 'I get paralysed if I don't know why; if I don't have
a strong why, I'm useless.'

- Optimistic – my great friends David Grayson, Mark Lee
and Chris Coulter partnered with me to reach our combined network of chief sustainability officers, CSR leaders and changemakers with a survey for this book. One
stand-out insight from that survey, which was reflected
in my interviews, was how optimistic Solutionists are
(Figure 2.2). These are people whose vision is not of
'less bad' in the world but of visionary 'more good'.

FIGURE 2.2   Q: As an individual, do you consider yourself to be:

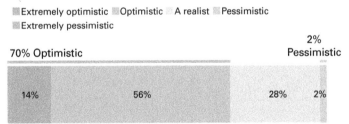

Source: GlobeScan, ERM's SustainAbility Institute and Futerra. The survey was offered
in English and completed in September 2022. It was completed by 50 sustainability
experts.

- Informed – no Solutionist is a 'Pollyanna' in their optimism. They aren't blindly optimistic and they are actually aware of the alternative track towards disaster that we could take. These are people deeply knowledgeable about the topics they invent solutions for – from climate change to social exclusion, systemic racism to biodiversity loss. Their expertise on the problems, yet their focus on solutions, reminded me often of this quote from Rachel Carson, who arguably sparked much of the modern environmental movement with her 1962 book *Silent Spring*:

> We stand now where two roads diverge. But unlike the roads in Robert Frost's familiar poem, they are not equally fair. The road we have long been travelling is deceptively easy, a smooth superhighway on which we progress with great speed, but at its end lies disaster. The other fork of the road — the one less travelled by — offers our last, our only chance to reach a destination that assures the preservation of the earth. (Carson, 1963)

- Future focused – the metaphors Solutionists used for their visions were often very future orientated and active. Like Daniel Servitje Montull, the CEO of Grupo Bimbo, said, 'You need a compass to the future, and that, at the end of the day, is what drives most of the people who are successful.' Ezgi Barcenas, Chief Sustainability Officer (CSO) of AB Inbev, put it as simply as, 'Vision pulls you forward.' Solutionists look to the future and imagine what is possible, not what is threatened. As one of my favourite quotes, often attributed to Nelson Mandela, reads, 'It always feels impossible until it's done.'

The point of grit

Hard work – was anything ever achieved without it? In Chapter 4 on the Mississippi mind, we'll explore how to nurture that tenacity in yourself and survive the drive that fills every Solutionist. Because, without exception, every Solutionist is:

- Committed – they are bound to their course. I can't imagine any of them dropping sustainability for another career.
- Driven – many felt compelled to create solutions. These are relentless people. I loved the observation by Karen Pflug, the CSO of IKEA, that, 'If we have all the big ideas and this wonderful purpose and vision, but don't bloody well get on with it, then what's the point?'
- Resilient – they aren't easily broken and they recover quickly from setbacks.
- Hard-working – their endurance is very impressive (in Chapter 10 on joyful entrepreneurship we'll discover the importance of stopping, sometimes).

As Chief Corporate Responsibility Officer of L'Oréal, Alexandra Palt, puts it: 'Grit and tenacity are essential in this career. I learnt that, as a woman standing up for difficult issues such as human rights, you must persevere and act independently of the resistance you meet.'

The point of flex

As US leader, Robert F Kennedy, said, 'Only those who dare to fail greatly can ever achieve greatly' (1966).

Compared to vision and grit, I feel like flexibility is an overlooked aspect of leadership, yet completely universal in every Solutionist story. In Chapter 4, we'll explore this ability to flex to circumstances and keep your eye on the vision.

All Solutionists:

- Are inventive – they are original thinkers who can see problems laterally to discover solutions.
- Fail fast – as Paul Polman, former CEO of Unilever, puts it, 'Continue to make more mistakes than do good things, because ultimately, that's how you develop as a person.' Throughout this book Solutionists share, sometimes with some relish, their glorious failures.
- Learn – both through study and experience, Solutionists take on new knowledge and insights. Bill Gates told me about a 'decades-long learning process' he went through with climate experts Ken Caldeira and David Keith:

  Up to six times per year, we'd have a half-day learning session. I would either learn from them or they would bring in other experts who would cover areas like how weather will be impacted by climate change in the future, what this means for agriculture, what exists now in terms of different energy-storage technologies, how cheap wind and solar energy could get and more. I would read a few hundred pages of material ahead of time; they would present and then we'd discuss the technology or issue. I loved these sessions. It's great to learn from a group of new experts.

- The most important part of this learning is that Solutionists change their mind when they learn something new.

- Adaptive – to context. Toni Petersson, the CEO of disruptive oat milk brand Oatly, explained to me that 'The world is changing every single day and you need to adapt to it in order to find solutions for it.' This ability to adjust and move fast is a skill, sometimes scary, but possible to learn.

The point of fun

When I asked author, entrepreneur and model Lily Cole what one piece of advice she would send back to her younger self, she replied, 'Don't be so hard on yourself. Have faith and enjoy the journey.'

For Solutionists, fun doesn't mean booze or balloons (well, sometimes it does). Despite the intense and overwhelming issues they deal with every day, Solutionists have a light-hearted, don't take yourself too seriously attitude. The stereotype of a social entrepreneur, or woke crusader in business, is of dour worthiness. There wasn't a drop of that in the people I interviewed and have worked with over the years. How does that manifest? Solutionists tend to:

- Enjoy work – Danny Alexander, one of the founders of the Who Gives A Crap toilet-paper unicorn, embodied this perfectly when he said to me, 'We're now at about almost 200 employees and distributing globally, and investing in a lot of new products, new distribution channels, and new marketing channels, so it's a pretty fun time!' Solutionists are busy, and they love it.
- Be candid – in these pages you're going to find swear words, forthright options and deeply personal stories.

Solutionists don't try cultivating an air of impressive distance. Being straightforward is necessary when working on the edge.

- Be collaborative – utterly committed to their own values, most Solutionists I spoke to sought to work with people outside their 'bubble'. Esther Speck, Vice President of Sustainable Business and Impact at Lululemon, explained it as, 'the most effective changemakers I've met find common ground with almost anyone.'
- Laugh – in every single interview, and in brainstorms about this book, in conferences to debate sustainability and in the Futerra offices – laughter always rings out. I don't know how to quote laughter, but the people who work on the world's most serious problems don't take themselves too seriously.

The point of soul

The word 'soul' isn't one you'll find in many business books, and I don't mean it in the religious sense. I needed a word powerful enough to convey the depth, importance and emotional power of Solutionists' faith that a better world is possible.

Every single one clearly sees the opportunities and welcomes the personal benefits and financial success which come from working in the Solutions Economy. However, the reason they do it is because they are moved to do so by a set of convictions woven into the fabric of their existence. For some, those beliefs came from childhood; others had an epiphany late in their career. As Vaitea Cowan, entrepreneur at hydrogen-energy start-up Enapter, explained to me, 'I don't know if I can even describe it, it's like my blood rushes to fulfil this purpose.'

How does this sense of 'soul' manifest? Solutionists are:

- Passionate – their eyes widen and their breathing speeds up; they lean forward with a focus you can feel radiating off them. This is a group of people who have been called 'intense' since they started working on solutions.
- Socially conscious – I wish there was a better phrase for this, but 'woke' has been pilloried and 'deeply concerned about social justice and environmental issues' wouldn't fit in the model. Simply put: every Solutionist is primarily motivated by making the world a better place.
- Activist – it's possible to be conscious, yet idle. Solutionists' social conscience is active and they are energetic in finding answers. More and more are also activist in terms of campaigning for social and environmental justice issues and intersectional sustainability.
- Has a calling – 'having a sense of purpose' is the modern way of saying 'having a calling'. I'm using the older, more soulful term, as the world's problems do seem to 'call' to Solutionists. They can't ignore them or hope someone else solves them.

Wangarĩ Muta Maathai was a Kenyan social, environmental and political activist and the first African woman to win the Nobel Peace Prize. Her life and achievements are an inspiration to so many Solutionists today, including myself. She put the 'soul' of being a Solutionist in beautifully direct words, 'I don't really know why I care so much. I just have something inside me that tells me that there is a problem, and I have got to do something about it' (1991).

Why do Solutionists care so very much?

While this Solutionist star explains *how* to be a Solutionist, we also need to understand *why* they are like that in the first place.

The itch to answer

If Hollywood made a movie of your life, what would be the key scenes from your origin story?

I asked this question of the Solutionists I interviewed for this book. The question matters because if Solutionists are just 'born that way', then there's not much point writing a book about how to become one. Over the decades of working with changemakers in every sector and industry, I've seen such a diversity of journeys – I'm convinced that Solutionists can be made.

That's the point of the Solutionist star: it gives you a template to begin building up your Solutionist muscles and balancing your skills. That takes work, so it helps to identify why you're doing so.

Many years ago, I had the pleasure of meeting a prototype Solutionist – one of the first business leaders to have that moment, that spark, that led him to set a clear vision at the top of his star.

Ray Anderson was the archetypal entrepreneur. In 1973 he had invented carpet tiles, so beloved of corporate offices. Despite some investors calling him crazy, 'Why would you want to cut a perfectly good carpet into squares?', he'd built his business, Interface, into a publicly traded company. By 1994, Ray was 60, a millionaire CEO and perfect example of the American dream.

Then he was asked to give the sales force at Interface some talking points about the company's approach to the environment – because customers had started to ask.

'That's simple,' Mr. Anderson recalled thinking. 'We comply with the law.'

Legal compliance being a poor sales tool (and dull fodder for a speech), he started reading up about environmental issues, especially waste mountains and the impacts of the petroleum his invention was made of: 'I was running a company that was plundering the earth,' he realized. 'I thought, "Damn, someday people like me will be put in jail!"' (2007). 'It was a spear in the chest.'

Remember, this was in the mid-90s when the terms 'sustainability', 'ESG' or 'restorative business' would have raised bemused eyebrows in most CEOs. But Ray challenged Interface to become such a 'restorative enterprise', a sustainable operation that takes nothing out of the earth that cannot be recycled or quickly regenerated, and that does no harm to the biosphere.

The first time he pitched that sustainability message to a group of Wall Street investors, the outcome wasn't welcome: 'The next day our analyst called to say that one of our biggest investors was dumping the stock because he had clearly gone "round the bend".'

Thankfully, Ray reframed the challenge to make it part of his job as CEO to be 'round the bend' so he could see what was coming up next. He knew that bringing the Interface team along would take more than inspirational speeches. So, he tied the top teams' bonuses to sustainability metrics – swiftly leading to massive cuts in waste and substantial financial savings.

Not everything delivered an immediate win–win. Interface sold off any flooring products deemed unsustainable, to concentrate on the production of carpet tiles that could be recycled and replaced. That initially tanked the share price, but then new investors came onboard, who believed in the opportunity of reaping the benefits of a brand-new innovation-based positioning. Within a few months, the stock price reached an all-time high.

Today, Interface is engaged in a new strategy – Climate Take Back – with the overarching goal of becoming a carbon-negative company by 2040 – and they launched the world's first carbon-negative carpet tiles in 2020.

When Ray passed away, some years ago, his legacy was assured.

Although his story is extraordinary, thankfully, it's no longer unique. In 2022, there are millions of leaders, entrepreneurs and changemakers who have had their own 'spear through the heart' moment. For this book, I've studied those experiences, to see if they can be replicated to spark more awesome changemakers within business and across society. Through my interviews and surveys, I've discovered there are three ways that an 'itch' to create change can be triggered:

- Childhood experiences – just under half of those I've interviewed and surveyed can recall a 'core memory' from youth that set their feet on this path.
- Life-changing moments – only 15% of Solutionists experienced a life-altering event, but many of those who did are the most fervent in their search for answers.

- Thoughtful reflections – around one-third discovered a passion for change mid- or late career (much like Ray Anderson did) through research and thinking about the world we live in.

Solutionist from the start

For Kate Brandt, who heads up Google's global sustainability efforts, her moment is one of her earliest memories:

> I have one very distinct memory from when I was small, I don't know from exactly when, probably 4 or 5 years old. There was this beautiful stand of eucalyptus trees on my drive into school, and I loved to watch them. Then, one morning, workers started felling those trees. Every day, I watched as more were cut down, until a several-acre part of the forest was simply gone – built over with tarmac. I was absolutely devastated, and my parents remember me crying for days. Today I know those eucalyptus trees weren't native to the area so removing them wasn't the brutal attack I thought it was as a child. But back then, for me, it was like, 'This is a beautiful part of the natural world that's been in my daily life', and then I saw how quickly it could go away if we didn't take care of it.

Kate went on to advise the US Navy on energy efficiency and worked in the Obama administration as the United States' first federal chief sustainability officer. Under her watch, Google has become the world's largest purchaser of renewable energy, and is pioneering ways to identify, and map, deforestation across the world.

That story is mirrored by hydrogen-energy entrepreneur Vaitea Cowan, who had her 'itch' to change things triggered after experiencing smog for the first time:

> I was born in New Caledonia, a paradise island in the South Pacific, with a large family and strong connection to the beautiful natural environment we lived in. Then I moved to Thailand, because I heard wonderful things about the nature, the culture, the people and the food of Chiang Mai. But when I moved there, I breathed heavy smog for the first time. I'd never experienced air pollution, never had it impair my eyesight and crawl in my lungs. For the first time I was breathing air that wasn't clean. I was already aware of climate change because my home island is threatened by it. But it was no longer this 'My island is in danger because of the sea level rise' that I had read about through the IPCC reports. Smog was something I felt, rather than thought about. In that moment my childhood love for the environment shifted into 'I have to do something about this, now.'

Last year, the firm she co-founded, Enapter, won the Earthshot Prize (a £1 million grant awarded for outstanding environment impact, founded by Prince William in 2021). Her magical technology is called the Anion Exchange Membrane (AEM) Electrolyser. It turns renewable electricity and water into low-cost green hydrogen, which can be used to power households or to power industry. The electrolysers are modular and stackable, so people and businesses can go as big or as small as they want. Crucially, it can replace the fuels and gases that currently make up 80 per cent of global energy consumption (Enapter, 2021). Enapter's technology is already used in 44 countries and across sectors from mobility to heating and telecommunications. Vaitea is adamant that in her lifetime, no one will have to breathe that polluted air again.

Many of us might have a similar memory of the nature we took for granted as a child being destroyed or polluted in ways that snapped us into doing something about it.

For some, the 'itch' came not from wanting to save nature, but from nature saving them, as farmer Leah Penniman explains:

> I was a multi-racial black child, one of three, growing up in rural Massachusetts in a very conservative, working-class town that did not approve of our family's presence. So, needless to say, school was a real struggle. To say that we were bullied would be an understatement. And my siblings and I found great solace in the forest, you know, the pine trees and the blueberries and winter berries. The squirrels on the perch, they became our friends and community and our support. So, from a very young age, I developed a fierce sense of commitment to the natural world as family. So, when I became a teen and needed my first real job, I chose to get a job at a farm and have been farming ever since. I completely fell in love with the elegant simplicity of seed and soil to harvest, feeding the community and caring for the earth at the same time.

Since 2010, Leah has run Soul Fire Farm in Grafton, New York. It's a black and indigenous-led non-profit which grows food organically across 80 acres of mountain land. It is centred on Afro-indigenous practices, drawing on ancestral knowledge of the best way to cultivate crops. The solace she found as a child has become the solution she works on as an adult.

These Solutionists were 'made' at an early age, and through this book we'll meet others who had their Solutionist itch triggered early. Sometimes by the smallest moment, like for Ezgi Barcenas, CSO of brewer AB Inbev, when she was five years old:

> I was in the kitchen, and I dropped an ice cube on the floor, so I picked it up and I tossed it in the garbage bin. My Dad was there, and he said, 'Hey, why did you put the ice cube in the garbage bin?' and I said 'Oh, it was dirty, it fell on the floor'. He frowned at me and said: 'Why don't you put it in a flowerpot?' I was raised in Cyprus where water scarcity was part of daily life. The need to save the water in an ice cube shook me awake about the problem.

Almost everyone I've spoken to or surveyed who had this 'awakening' in childhood has set themselves a Solutionist career from the get-go. As corporate changemakers, innovative entrepreneurs and even activists – each had their 'soul' part of their star in place before they'd barely started.

Of course, not everyone has a childhood epiphany, and sometimes it can take quite a shake to wake up to your own potential.

Life-changing moments

What I wasn't expecting, as I listened to the fascinating stories of Solutionists, was how many people pivot towards sustainability after major life traumas. For more than one of my interviewees, the 'spear through the heart' moment was as dramatic as the metaphor:

> Within my life, the biggest turning point was when I was 31 years old. I had a near-death experience, and for three weeks I was barely conscious. It was meningitis, and I barely survived. One thing that really changed when that happened was my concept of time. I always knew that I was going to die someday, of course. Suddenly, it became a fact that my life was indeed going to end one day, and I realized fully then that I have this very limited time in which to achieve what I want to achieve. Also, through the extraordinary care I received from my wife and the doctors, I realized there are people who can help – if I look for them. As I slowly recovered, I had time on my hands to think about just which pathway I should choose for the rest of my life. Please know, I didn't think about changing the world! One of my deciding factors is that if I choose this pathway, will that make me proud? If I don't choose this pathway, will I regret it later? I think if I can do that, I believe at the end of my life I can look back and say, 'I made the right decisions.'

Mr Yoshihiro Hasebe is CEO of Kao Corporation, the giant personal-care business headquartered in Japan. He told me this story to explain why his decisions for Kao's future are always about finding the balance between rising profits and falling environmental impact – in everything from shampoo to shower gel, baby-care to bathroom cleaning spray – because otherwise he wouldn't be able to answer the question his near-death experience set for him.

Henk Jan, the CEO of Tony's Chocalonely, had a very similar story. Despite their wildly different businesses and cultural experiences, I almost got their quotes mixed up:

> In 2013, I had a stroke. I couldn't talk for 7 months; it was hard to move. That type of experience, in psychology it's called a twice born. That year I felt reborn, and I needed to be more radical choosing the stuff that's really important. For me, that started with a couple of personal changes. So, every morning I look in the mirror and say, 'Am I proud of what I did yesterday?' And 'Am I happy with what I'm going to do today?' It's just a little check-in with myself. And then, and I'm not sure that the word 'arrogance' is the right word, but having the balls to actually say, 'Well, if the answer is not yes, then I will change it immediately.'

Life-altering experiences can have world-altering effects, and you may be one of the people who have faced that moment.

Those leaders I spoke to who lived through these extremes were often 'normal' businesspeople before that. They might have been concerned about social and environmental issues, and even been ambitious and competent leaders. Crisis changed them into Solutionists.

Thoughtful change

Perhaps the most relatable pathway to becoming a Solutionist is simply deciding to be so and then making it happen. This was the route of IKEA's CEO Jesper Brodin:

> My first assignment with IKEA, in 1995, was in Karachi, Pakistan. I found out years later that the reason they took

somebody with no experience of working abroad, and putting me in Pakistan was because nobody else had applied for the job. But it was a fascinating experience. There were great business opportunities, I was working with amazing people, but at the same time there were deeply troubling environmental and social issues. And as a young manager, I wasn't given enough guidance for making the right decisions. That experience convinced me that IKEA needed a code of conduct – clear directions, with consequences, for making good business decisions for society and the environment. That code, it took us 10 years to implement it globally, across all our supply chain. The starting point was scary, as managers asked, 'Would costs go up? Would it be possible? Are we morally responsible for something outside our own company walls, in our values chain? What about respecting other cultures' ways of working?' It was a phenomenal debate. In the end, we said, 'We have to. We can't be ourselves and represent our values in IKEA unless we let that reflect on the people and our planet.' It wasn't easy, as you can imagine, there were all sorts of technicalities, disagreements and headaches. But we managed to not only make IKEA and our partners a better place, and we also influenced a lot of people. At the end of the day, it's a beautiful outcome because the quality is better, our costs are better, our efficiency is better, and our factories are more competitive. It was super good for business, and super good for people and planet.

This is a story I've heard from CEOs and entrepreneurs across the world. At some point in their career, they stopped, looked around them, and decided what they saw simply wasn't good enough. For some, it was reading about the threat of climate change, or the brutal realities of modern slavery. Others visited somewhere in the world experiencing the costs of unsustainable business practices. Arguments with your kids about your job can spark a 'soul' moment. Or the nightly drumbeat of news about our fracturing systems can be enough.

In truth, having an itch to answer the world's questions is all it takes to be a Solutionist. Becoming a *successful* Solutionist takes a little more work.

The first step, as the ancient Greek philosophers said, is 'Know Thyself'.

EXERCISE   Solutions starters

I hope that as you read through these stories, a memory, or even more than one, floated to the surface.

If you're still searching for that itch, there's a way to find your motivating factor.

- Ask yourself: what is it about how the world runs that really pisses you off?

You'll know what that is because it's an issue, topic, product or policy that you've been drawn into arguments about more than once. It's the thing that over a beer, if the topic arises, you lean forward and say, 'Look, the thing is about that...'

Many of the world's greatest solutions have come about not because of calm reflection, but from a deep annoyance and the sense that someone just won't put up with things staying the same way as they have before.

Chapter 6 on 'Hope is a business plan' includes further triggers, topics and sectors ripe for change.

CHAPTER THREE

Architects, Accelerators and Actioners

We've all sat through the meeting. The one where a 'big-picture thinker' scribbles across a flipchart explaining how global trends are converging in a way few have noticed – revealing an exciting opportunity. Everyone's leaning forward, grasping at the threads the speaker is weaving together, and a bold new idea begins to form…

Then, the speaker pulls in a few more conceptual strands, wanders off down one of them, relates the entire thing to some obscure scientific or cultural concept and, eventually, they start to sound like a mad professor.

That's me. I'm a big-picture 'architect' who's happiest finding new solutions by noticing meta-pattens in global phenomena. Over the years, I've watched people slump back from an early fascination with an insight I've presented, to then fall into catatonic zombiedom as I just… kept… talking.

That's taught me, the hard way, that while all Solutionists embody the five aspects of the star – vision, grit, flex, fun and soul – those stars are in very different orbits.

For this book, I surveyed hundreds of successful start-up eco-entrepreneurs. They include the first fair-trade plastic recycler, an innovator making solar panels without glass and a battery manufacturer storing energy in ice. I had to check my survey findings more than once because their responses blew my expectations. Perhaps rather self-indulgently, I'd assumed many of them would be like me – big-picture horizon-focused folks. Instead, the founders of these growing businesses embody different leadership approaches, preferences and skills. Among all the survey data, and interviews, I've identified three, very distinct, types of Solutionist: the Architect, the Accelerator and the Actioner.

Each starts with an 'A' because all three have much in common with the notorious 'Type A' personality that is often bandied about in business circles. This personality stereotype was proposed by two cardiologists in the 1950s to describe the ambitious, driven, overworked and intense types of people who tended back then to require a cardiologist's attention. Being a Type A isn't a bed of roses – workaholism, impatience and competitiveness can become overwhelming – that's why in Chapter 10 on joyful entrepreneurship I've set out how to self-care the Solutionist way. I don't mind if you resonate with the 'Type A' resemblance, or consider yourself a 'Type B' or 'Type-less' person. All that matters is that Architects, Accelerators and Actioners each have their own special superpowers, a set of abilities and perspectives that mean they can do what others can't.

If you can identify your 'A', it will accelerate your effectiveness as you lean into your gifts and dodge your limitations.

You'll also benefit from understanding, valuing and learning how to collaborate with the other types. In fact, that might be even more important for your success than understanding yourself. Because the problems we face, from social injustice to climate change, are non-linear and you often must create the solutions as you go. Having a team made up of only Actioners can be very effective in businesses that have honed their process to perfection and now just need to get it done. Team-building Accelerators are brilliant at recruiting, motivating and directing people towards a goal, and teams of Architects function brilliantly as think-tanks pumping out ideas into the world. However, to invent, transform or do something new – that takes all three Solutionist types working together. I can't imagine a sustainability challenge that won't require that, or a successful business that doesn't already do it.

Which type of Solutionist are you?

Read through the following portraits and reflect on which you vibe with most. Many of the Solutionists who have reviewed these pages told me that the 'How it goes wrong' sections are the most helpful – because many of us recognize our shortcomings more swiftly than our strengths.

You also need to be able to recognize, understand and cherish the other types, because you're going to need their help.

1. The Architects

Architects see the biggest possible picture. They zoom out to look at the outline of things and how they fit together. They see a problem in terms of the structures that surround it and the interconnecting systems that bring it about. Their stars shine bright in 'vision' and intellectual 'flexibility', but can struggle with the soft skills in their 'fun' point.

HOW DO ARCHITECTS WORK?

Given the problem of, say, too much waste being created during the manufacturing of a product, Architects will find solutions in far-ranging places: as well as simply reducing the amount of waste, they might ask how they can turn the waste product into a new product altogether, or how the waste could be used by another industry as a useful raw material. They'll review every option – including whether the waste can be designed out by transforming the raw-material sourcing.

Linear plans aren't their strong suit. Like a real-life architect, they can see the building, but not the people inside. They like big statistics and sweeping, high-level views; they don't resonate with anecdotes or anomalies. They prefer binoculars to microscopes.

Jacques-Julien Rième, Insights Director at Electrolux, embodied this perspective when he called for Solutionists to 'have an engineer mindset that understands the order of magnitudes in progress to be made. Focus on the bigger picture, the impactful things rather than dissipate into greenwashing shiny things.'

This big-picture thinking doesn't mean Architects aren't well evidenced or missing specifics – in fact they are adept at handling huge amounts of information and translating that into a grand theory of everything. Many of the Architects I've met over the years make great dinner-party conversationalists, hopping from topic to topic with fascinating bites of information. Yet, they might forget to ask your name, or about your actual life, because they only want to know what you think. Nothing pleases an Architect more than noticing an unexpected corollary, unfilled gap in solutions or lateral opportunity. As leaders, the best of them surround themselves with Accelerators and Actioners who can inspire teams and make things happen. And, they seek out other Architects to kick the tyres of their ideas and enjoy 'meta-think' with.

WHEN IT GOES RIGHT

Few companies have a chief sustainability officer with the credentials of Dr Emma Stewart of Netflix. A trained environmental scientist with years of research under her belt, Emma was part of the team which literally developed the world's first science-based climate-target methodology.

She admits she wasn't a huge TV addict before joining Netflix but was fascinated by the opportunity to bring a science-based approach to sustainability across Netflix's creative portfolio. Swiftly working through the company's operational footprint, she designed a net-zero strategy which moved Netflix from a laggard to a leader.

Emma is an Architect extraordinaire, and realized the environmental footprint was only half the story. Because Netflix also has a cultural footprint, she likes to explain it as 'really being a window to the world through storytelling that travels across boundaries and across cultures'.

In true Architect fashion, Emma sourced the facts. Her team meticulously combed through Netflix's entire slate of content, identifying programmes like *Down to Earth with Zac Efron* or films like the Oscar-winning *My Octopus Teacher* as stories with strong sustainability themes. They found that 165 million households around the world had watched at least one of their many environmentally themed titles in 2020. This proved to creators inside Netflix that there was an appetite for more shows like that. The climate-analogy movie *Don't Look Up* with Leonardo di Caprio came out soon after, and busted records for viewership.

Emma also gathered an advisory group of experts from around the world, including climate scientists, youth activists and experts in storytelling, both to advise and provoke Netflix on using its incredible reach to generate the stories that generate change. The result is a very clear overarching strategy based on the logical premise that: 'Netflix exists to entertain the world, and that requires a habitable world to entertain.'

Today, you can visit a unique sustainability channel on Netflix (do so, it will improve your recommendations), and the world's go-to 'chill' platform has been working to 'flip the script' on sustainability creativity away from dystopias and towards solutions.

Using her scientific Architect skills, Emma has made space for creativity to shine. She likes to quote the scientist Peter Kareiva by saying, 'Science tells us what to do, while storytelling makes us want to do it.'

WHEN IT GOES WRONG

As an Architect myself, I know the problems we face only too well.

When Architects are stressed or overwhelmed, they can 'spin' into a weird obsessive Actioner – becoming hyper-fixated on details. This isn't their strong point, so they aren't effective as changemakers on that level. Architects are very used to making compelling and even aggressive cases for their big-picture visions. Apply that passion to small stuff – and they can make every tiny detail feel like a life/death issue for their colleagues, their teams and themselves.

The scale of their thinking can also be difficult to get out of their heads and into other people's. Especially in sustainability, so many of the 'threads' they are drawing upon might be only just emerging, therefore not yet well recognized or widely understood. If Architects don't lay the groundwork for their ideas, making sure everyone understands the backstory, then their solutions can sound wackier than they actually are. Too often, Architect leaders rely on their teams trusting them to know the direction the world is moving in, rather than working to articulate that clearly so they aren't the only one who can see the horizon.

Architects can burn out with frustration when they can't see change. An 'on-the-ground' Actioner sees the impact they make immediately, but change at the satellite level that Architects operate in can take decades, or even lifetimes, to materialize. Working alongside Actioners can keep Architects sane and connected to the real world.

Beyond business, I've met many Architect Solutionists in academia. They are also great medical diagnosticians, legal judiciaries, strategists, inventors, writers and, of course, architects.

HOW TO BE AN EFFECTIVE ARCHITECT

- Find Accelerators and Actioners who value working with you; they'll bring the social and completer skills to balance your star.
- Don't 'tell' people, but instead try to engage people in your big-picture vision – perhaps others might even enhance the idea.
- Keep your Actioner 'shadow-side' fed. Volunteer, dig a garden, build something. It will keep you grounded and teach you how real work works.
- Work on your communications skills and ability to articulate clearly. There's little point having a vision for a new building if you can't draw a blueprint for it to be built.
- Stay involved. Architects occasionally walk away when the project/business/solution is up and running. You do need to let the Accelerators and Actioners do their job – just be available to them. If they hit a snag, then going back to the original vision will help – so you might be needed.
- Watch out for what's next. Seeing the whole picture is your gift – so take that responsibility to find the next solution.

2. The Accelerators

If Architects think in terms of systems, Accelerators care all about culture. Their superpower is to curate super-teams, and act as the central pivot that holds everyone together. They see the psychological angle of any situation and know how to get the best out of everyone involved. They look at how people fit in and fit together, and they act as the glue between them all. Those team-building and warmth skills in the 'fun' point of the star come easily to Actioners, but their 'vision' point can be in need of burnishing.

HOW DO ACCELERATORS WORK?

Accelerators' work can sometimes feel like where the 'magic' happens, because it's less visible or logic-based than that of others. They can make a group feel – and act – like a unit and achieve more than they knew was possible.

While an Architect will see how the bigger machinery of the business needs to change, an Accelerator will get everyone on board with the changes. They might ask, how are we going to tell this story? Are all the right people on board? Who are we missing on this team? Does everyone know how, and feel empowered, to do what's needed? Can we bring in lateral skills? Accelerators bet on passionate individuals and well-designed teams who can make anything possible. They're adept at internal politics, brilliant at socializing ideas and tend to have a strong network of allies inside and outside any organization.

Connection is their modus operandi; they listen well and have a Spidey-sense for how individuals and groups are feeling. Technical processes and detailed practicalities may not be their strong suit – but they will find and motivate the right team to action anything.

WHEN IT GOES RIGHT

Entreprenuer Kevin Song has a motto written in permanent marker pen on a whiteboard in his office: 'A company is just a collection of people.'

He explained to me why: 'People often forget that's what a company is – just a group of hard-working individuals who are inspired by some idea and want to work to actually put that idea into motion. So, I think for me it all comes back to the people and whether I can impact the people that I'm working with by giving them a great sense of purpose and great incentives and compensation and figuring out how to be the best employer. Then I think you can solve any problem or any mission.'

Kevin founded withco, a groundbreaking new property-ownership platform for small businesses. He was inspired to build the business because when his parents arrived in the United States from South Korea, they had little to their name. Within a few years, they had managed to buy a grocery store in Brooklyn, New York. They and their shop became an important part of the local community, sponsoring Little League games and being ambassadors for the neighbourhood. Then one day, a phone call from their new landlord changed everything: their rent had doubled. The business couldn't survive such a dramatic financial hit and was forced to close just weeks later.

Song has never forgotten what happened to his family's business and wanted to find a way to protect others from suffering the same fate. Many small business owners find that it's significantly easier to secure a lease than a mortgage, leaving them stuck in expensive rental arrangements. To solve this, withco finds and buys commercial real estate that houses existing small businesses, then places the tenants on equity-building, lease-to-own plans. Small business owners continue to pay rent, but as they do so they also build equity in the property and have the option to purchase the property down the line at a pre-agreed price. This means their rent payment is no longer simply lining developers' pockets, and instead puts them on the path towards ownership. These are people-led businesses, and Kevin's leadership philosophy reflects that:

> There's a real conflict sometimes between your individualistic sense of driving change as the founder of the company and your team's ability to drive that. I want to keep realigning myself to always remember that my main stakeholder that I should be taking care of is actually not the customer, it should be the team, and that the team will eventually take care of the customer. I'd like to see more CEOs really taking care of their people. I think that, as part of the late-stage capitalism thing, that we've all sort of forgotten that there used to be an era where mid-sized businesses really took care of their people.

Those are exactly the type of businesses that withco supports. Launched in 2019, by 2022 withco was on track to help 100 small businesses. All are carefully assessed to ensure that they are healthy enough, and suitable for, taking on property ownership. And withco provides financial business consulting support to every business that goes through the process, to help them make the transition. In 2022, withco raised $32 million from venture firms as well as celebrities including Venus Williams and Will Smith.

It's no hyperbole to say that Kevin puts his team's success as the foundation of his own: 'I hope the thing I would be remembered for the most, is that I have directly impacted my people and they have experienced real positive change in their lives for whatever gives them meaning – that would be enough.'

WHEN IT GOES WRONG

Accelerators suffer when their team is disjointed, unhappy or underperforming. Their deep loyalty to their people can tempt them to blame processes, structures and outside factors rather than confront problems of underperformance or poor personal dynamics within their circle.

At their best, they can overcome those challenges, but when overwhelmed or overworked they will suffer significant angst on behalf of their staff – sometimes more than the team itself is feeling.

The best Accelerators mentor, coach and uplift people to get things done. Underexperienced or overstretched Accelerators can become defensive, protecting their teams from feedback and fighting their battles for them even if their people would be happy to take the heat. This can have an infantilizing effect – creating a team of dependants rather than independent high-performers. Taking a step back and watching who steps up can act as a circuit breaker for Accelerators who have become overprotective.

Fairness and equity are superpowers of Accelerators and, as social justice becomes ever more central to sustainability, Accelerators must lead the diversifying of the talent taking on these huge issues. Doing so demands that Accelerators tackle their own biases. Because human connections and 'vibe' matter greatly to them, it can blind Accelerators to the fact they've built a team of 'people like them'. Those teams might be comfortable for the Accelerator but when it comes to our sustainable future, that's not what we need.

Many of the most effective Solutionists I work with are Accelerators. There are communities of change, networks, businesses and campaigns all created, built and led by Accelerators. What constantly surprises me is how often they talk themselves down. Because people are their power, they can denigrate their own sustainability/technical knowledge, especially when comparing themselves to the academic 'vision-heavy' Architects. Because they enabled others rather than 'doing the stuff' themselves like Actioners, they too often belittle their contribution. I've had enough of it! Without Accelerators nothing would get done, so take your power – you are expert and impactful – and we need you.

Accelerators make great teachers, salespeople, networkers and fundraisers, coaches, military leaders and even politicians.

HOW TO BE AN EFFECTIVE ACCELERATOR

- Hold the space for magic to happen between people.
- Curate spaces of welcoming, creativity and trust between unlikely allies and groups unfamiliar with each other.

- Many people feel confused and even intimidated by the social justice and environmental agenda. You are comfortable with honesty, so open up about how you overcame your own barriers to action, which will bring more people in.
- Spot the Architects you want to work with. In a perfect partnership your Architect will inspire the 'vision' point of your star. They will likely have great ideas for the big levers of technology, finance and policy, and plans to get them done. However, they will have forgotten that nothing happens without people.
- Surround yourself with mentors – including people younger than you and from different perspectives and backgrounds from your own.
- Rethink 'diversity and inclusion' as 'diversity and belonging'. Belonging in a team means more than just being included in it. Accelerators generate a sense that everyone is wanted, needed and important in the team. Make sure that ability is spread widely and fairly.
- You learn from people rather than learning from paperwork – so make sure you always have someone to 'talk it through' with.
- Plan. Too often Accelerators will rely on their strong people skills to see them through, but for big sustainability projects you need a proper plot.
- People like you, and that feels great! This is such a superpower in keeping teams going through rough patches and bringing out the best in people. Please remember, some decisions are necessarily unlikeable and will put strains on relationships. Bring in your Architects and

Actioners for those moments – they'll have the objectivity to get you through.
- We need more Solutionists – and you're our best recruiter!

3. The Actioners

Actioners are all about, you guessed it: taking action. When they see a problem – whether in their community, in society or at work – they're the first to get their hands dirty, fixing it there and then. Always practical and 'can do', they move fast and make things happen. If they like a plan – they'll turn it into reality. In the next chapter, we'll explore the Actioners' superpower on the star, 'grit', but also their weak spot of 'flex'.

HOW DO ACTIONERS WORK?

Actioners' problem solving is direct and on the spot. If project management and organization has become a problem at work, they'll leap into action with time management tools and training for everyone on the team. Or if recycling rates in the office are too low, they'll jump to the task of installing new recycling bins and making signs. If product development is held up because of a supplier, they'll find a new one.

Actioners see the problem – and its solution – in terms of its immediate context. That's how they can move so quickly and act so decisively. They are invaluable to any Solutionist organization – they turn questions into answers and possibilities into realities.

Their curiosity is centred on the pragmatic, the 'how'. They see obstacles as challenges to climb over, round or through, and they are laser focused on achieving tangible objectives. Actioners often love working with Architects – they appreciate (but wouldn't themselves enjoy) the intellectual knots that Architects tie themselves up in finding a breakthrough idea/insight/invention. When the answer, finally, pops out, the Actioner gets to make it happen with all the completer-finisher satisfaction that comes from doing things. Actioners also work well with Accelerators, especially those who connect them to other Actioners. Because they know most big projects can't get done by one person – and being part of an effective and impactful team consistently ticking off the 'to do' list – that's an Actioner's happy place.

WHEN IT GOES RIGHT

Jamie Palmer is very much a hands-on Actioner. In his first year of launching Social Supermarket his team received orders for about 700 gift-boxes of his ethical and sustainable treats. Each one was exciting to pack up and Jamie often tracked them through from order to dispatch.

Then Covid-19 hit and people in lockdown were all searching online for fun and unusual gifts that would be appreciated by people stuck at home – and Social Supermarket's orders jumped to 13,000 almost overnight. To put that in context, in the last three months of the business's first year, they made 95 per cent of their revenue. Their fulfilment centre, already hit by Covid sick days and social distancing, couldn't handle the capacity. Perhaps someone else would have sent refunds and apologies to those customers who wouldn't get their Christmas order.

Jamie and his business partners asked their friends and family to help, and they hand-packed over 2,000 hampers over the course of two weekends. I know that Jamie is an Actioner not just because he did it, but because he was grinning telling me the story of long days (and nights) lugging boxes, stripping shelves of organic cookies, chutneys and chocolates, and folding up mountains of cardboard.

This is Jamie's gift, and his joy – seeing and feeling the impact he is making. Because he mainly works with small businesses that supply the goodies in his gift-boxes:

> When we have a big sale, and can sell a significant amount of their products, we tangibly hear back what the feedback is and the growth of their business. We have one brand that provides employment for refugees, and we've worked with them over the past three years. I think in our first year we sold about 20 per cent of their total sales! I'd never take credit for their success, but seeing that significant impact is motivating. Those sales helped fund their first café in London staffed by refugees. For me, that's wow.

Working 'hands-on' rather than 'high-up' keeps Jamie going. 'I get to see the tangible impact that even small sales have, whereas, if we were selling that product for a multinational wholesaler, well, that company wouldn't even notice a difference.'

WHEN IT GOES WRONG

Actioners don't like twiddling their thumbs. In times of uncertainty, lack of direction or when action needs to be paused while problems are 'talked through', Actioners can become very uncomfortable, then frustrated and even exasperated. Why do we have to go over all this again, let's just do something!

While the Actioner's can-do attitude is awesome, sometimes things really do need to be discussed, chewed over and looked at from all sides. The Actioner's impatience might lead to hasty decisions or actions with less impact. Many of the most effective Actioners I've worked with have great strategies for those moments – they'll contribute their thoughts and then excuse themselves from the discussion, going off to get other things done. Others have cultivated patience with the process, often making lots of notes of possible actions during meetings and debates rather than jumping in with them.

At worst, Actioners can become rudderless machines that plough on regardless – doing thing after thing even as the effectiveness of action drops – because stopping doing something feels worse than doing something wrong.

Actioners also must learn delegation, but that doesn't always come naturally, which is why working with Accelerators can be so productive for Actioners. Accelerators are team builders and love to see people develop, learn and grow. They help Actioners see the potential in team members whom the Actioner might not have noticed in their own drive to 'do, do, do'. This skill is what separates the Actioners who become leaders and Solutionists in their own right from those who play 'safe pairs of hands' within a team but never get given responsibility for larger things.

Just because stuff needs doing, even if it 'itches' until it's done, although it's sitting there just waiting to be picked up – you might not be the right person to do it. In sustainability this happens again and again. Well-meaning and dedicated Actioners see a problem in society – someone is hungry, injustice is rife, people need help – and they jump in to solve it. As we're all learning, those 'saviour' mindsets don't always save, and can even worsen a situation. I'm not saying don't do anything about the horrible injustices and environmental emergencies you see; just go and find Actioners who are already there – from the community that's being impacted. This can be hard for Actioners because it takes them one step back from where things are happening – so it's not your hand that is helping. The mature Actioner is a smart Solutionist and knows the outcome matters more than the process.

It can be immensely satisfying to see the fruits of your labours, and Actioners get a fulfilment that Architects rarely do because Actioners can see a direct line from their work to real impact in the world. Outside the business sector, sustainability is very well served by Actioners working in global aid and crisis response, healthcare and first responders, engineering and practical sciences, creatives and designers, and anywhere that good stuff needs doing.

HOW TO BE AN EFFECTIVE ACTIONER

- You are an impact-making, real-world-shaking, get-things-done powerhouse! Make sure all that completer-finisher energy is cleverly pointed at the biggest impact you can make. A friendly Architect can help you with that.
- Stop, reflect, change. You can be so busy doing things, you might not always be learning from them. That 'flex' point of your star might need some attention. Schedule in reflection time, sit down with a notebook and write

out what worked, what didn't, and why, about your last project. Then decide what will change next time. Treat reflection itself like a task – set goals and a standard to judge when you've 'completed' this round of reflection. Too often reflection is advertised as passive, so Actioners aren't always attracted to the practice. So, make it another thing you simply must get done correctly and effectively.

- Are you the right person in the right place at the right time? Actioners need to ask themselves this question more often. If you see problems, there's probably already someone trying to solve it, and the best action you can take is to lift them up.
- Seek out the Accelerators and ask them to connect you to other Actioners! There are learning, tools, answers and insights just waiting for you from all the millions of other Actioners changing the world.
- Practise the skills every Actioner needs – patience, delegation and reflection. Master those and the things you're able to do will astound you.

How can I use this?

Whichever type of Solutionist you are, you are desperately needed. Architects, Accelerators and Actioners are all critical for making meaningful change in the world, and in business. Introducing new business models, inventing products and services, adapting your supply chain, investing in growth ideas, developing relationships with local communities, empowering under-represented groups in your workplace and society and making it all real – these all require thinking and acting that comes from all three angles.

Without an Architect, Accelerators and Actioners propel themselves towards unclear goals and spend a lot of energy treading water. With no Accelerators, Architects and Actioners move alone and can't reach their potential. And if there's no Actioner, well – very little gets done.

One of the most important things you can do as a Solutionist is define which type you are, then surround yourself with people who are different from you. Acknowledge your differences and embrace them. Learn to work together and maximize the unique strengths you each bring. Together, you make each other's Solutionist stars burn brighter.

EXERCISE Solutions starters

1 Draw a three-bubble Venn diagram and plot your network across it.

2 Folks whom you're confident are an Architect, Accelerator or Actioner – write them into their respective bubble.

3 Some people might be a mix of more than type, so they go into the cross-over spaces in the Venn. Make sure you have a large enough piece of paper because you need to delve deep and remember as many colleagues, contacts and friends as you can!

Some people who have effectively used this practice dedicate different colours for their direct team, and then other groups who are vital to them – investors, critics, competitors, allies and so on.

---

4   Then, place yourself on the Venn (written in a funky
    colour perhaps).

How is your map looking? Is your network well balanced?
How does your team look – is there a good spread of
Architects, Accelerators and Actioners?

Reading above, you've discovered your superpowers but
also your kryptonite. It's your network that can balance you
out. And you most definitely need mentors across all three
groups.

Some of the Solutionists I work with go a step further
and have utilized this model to map the entire stakeholder
universe on their issue – to help them to hone their 'ask' of
different people.

With a clear view of who you are, and the strengths of
those around you – your solution will be much more likely to
succeed.

CHAPTER FOUR

The Mississippi mind

The Mississippi river has been charting its course through a continent for at least 70 million years. To be more precise, the Mississippi river has been charting various 'courses' down from Lake Itasca to the Gulf of Mexico for all that time, because while the river has a firm source and an everlasting goal to reach the sea, it's been notoriously adaptable about how it gets between the two.

In a book about sustainability, I thought an ecosystem metaphor for part of the Solutionist star would be apt. Anyone who's travelled along its warm, powerful and unrelenting waterway might agree the grand Mississippi river is already a state of mind.

In my long career working in sustainability, moving from problem through to solution has never been linear, however much I might want it, just for once, to be. Much like the giant watercourse, Solutionists must meander a bit, feeling our way towards our ultimate goals. Erosion can dissolve paths we thought would work and silt can build up, blocking a way forward we had hoped would be easy.

However, as silt and sediment clog the river's main passage, the water rises, switching channels, finding a path that is steeper and more direct down to the Gulf of Mexico – pulled forward by the gravitational necessity of its goal. Some of those flexes in the path eventually become cut off from the rest of the river system and collect into little oxbow lakes. Rather than being wasted, many of these abandoned meanders evolve into marshland bursting with birds, insects and tall waving grasses.

This is the awesome power of adaptability, the wonderful art of trying-and-failing, and why flexibility is a skill every Solutionist must learn. The Mississippi mindset teaches that every twist and turn will help find the way to our destination, and that failures can create oxbow lakes with a richness and wildlife we might benefit from later.

The magic of changing your mind

Albert Einstein apocryphally once said that 'we cannot solve our problems with the same thinking we used when we created them' – and when it comes to being a Solutionist, he couldn't be more right.

So many of the problems we find ourselves in today spring from the same cradle – our take–make–use–waste manufacturing economy, exploitative employment structures, poverty-dependent commodities and the big bad of climate change. They stem from our ongoing loyalty to Victorian mercantile models and our dedication to maintaining them in a globalized and technological economy over 100 times larger than when those laws of capitalism were laid down.

A core attribute of Solutionists is how they dump useless approaches and swiftly flex to innovative ways of thinking. That speed and adaptability of thinking is desperately needed to build our new Solutions Economy.

You may be familiar with a famous puzzle involving a candle, some drawing pins and a box of matches? Your challenge is to mount the candle on the wall and light it. You try pinning the candle to the wall, but the wax is too hard and the pins too short. What do you do?

The answer requires us to overcome what German psychologist Karl Duncker called 'functional fixedness'. This is a type of cognitive bias that describes the human brain's tendency to see objects only in terms of the function we know them for. It's a shortcut that helps us cope with the vast amount of information in the world – but it's the enemy of creative problem solving.

So much of our current infrastructure, business models and social norms are functionally fixed, and the exploitation and destructive extraction they depend upon are similarly baked in. Solutionists are twisting themselves free of these outdated systems and daring to imagine functional fluidity and transformation.

The word 'solution' derives from the Latin 'solvere', which means to loosen, unbind and free. I couldn't have wished for a better etymological origin for us, because to be a Solutionist demands loosening assumptions, unbinding fixed problems and freeing imagination to flex into creativity.

Being aware of fixed function thinking is the first step to overcoming it. Once we do, we can remind ourselves to ask new questions of the problem in front of us and of the tools at our disposal. We can see a matchbox tray as a shelf, pin that to the wall, and light the candle sitting neatly on top of it.

Minds are made not born

Mississippi minds aren't fixed; they flex and are wonderfully (and occasionally alarmingly) open to thinking radically about the challenges we face. And sometimes, entire companies can have a 'Mississippi moment'.

Over 4,000 miles away from the great American river's vast meanderings, Danish energy company Ørsted did just that. Founded in the 1970s, the company spent the first half of its existence building coal-fired power plants and constructing huge oil and gas rigs in the seas around Europe. The company was called DONG, short for Danish Oil and Natural Gas, and was a successful business drawing in huge profits from fossil fuels.

Then, after one hell of a twist and an almighty turn, Ørsted became the world's most sustainable energy company. It has now built more offshore wind farms than any other developer in the world, creating enough offshore wind to power 9.5 million homes. It plans to triple this number by 2025. It has upended its business and completely changed the direction of its winding course.

This feat of adaptation was the result of changed minds. Ørsted (then DONG)'s leadership decided that they wanted to play a part in bringing down Denmark's embarrassingly high CO_2 emissions. In the early 2000s, Denmark was, as it still is, an exceptionally eco-conscious country. It introduced the world's first law on recycling in 1978, the world's first state-controlled 'organic' label in 1987, and the first tax on plastic bags in 1993. As the millennium turned, the Danish government set a target for renewables to make up 20 per cent of electric consumption by 2003. The country now aims to be 100 per cent fossil-fuel-free by at least 2050.

By leading a fossil-fuel company, the principals at DONG were running contrary to Danish culture and the expectation of Danes for energy independence. In 2004, DONG's leadership unveiled (to some shock and not a little scepticism) that the company would transform from 'black to green'. DONG started building offshore wind farms at pace, and soon shut down coal-fired plants and sold off oil and gas sites. With the capital from those sales, they reinvested in more offshore wind technology and construction.

In 2009, DONG adopted an 85/15 vision: the idea of switching from 85 per cent black and 15 per cent green, as the production then was, to the opposite. The then CEO, Anders Eldrup, announced that they would achieve this within a generation – a target the company would hit over 20 years ahead of schedule.

By 2017, DONG realized they had become too green for their name. They rebranded as Ørsted, after the Danish scientist Hans Christian Ørsted – the man who discovered the electromagnetism that renewable energy relies on. By 2023, Ørsted intends to be completely coal-free and to have reduced their CO_2 emissions by 96 per cent against a 2006 baseline.

It is a radical U-turn, an enormous bend in the river. How did they do it?

The first questions, and rather loud ones, came from shareholders. The fossil-fuel industries' biggest companies have, after all, made almost $2 trillion in profits in the past three decades. Shareholders challenged Ørsted's radical shift right from the start, and the company was nearly derailed by the high costs involved. Leadership stayed the course, determined that Ørsted could prove that environmental transformation and profitability can enhance each other. Taking advantage of the EU's and Denmark's own subsidies and incentives for wind power was an important part of this, so to reassure shareholders, leadership secured government assurances that those subsidies would stick around long enough for Ørsted to make the switch.

These financial moves were only part of the picture. They reflect something that runs much deeper in Ørsted and its leadership: the ability to adapt. Climate change, political change and culture change would, in the long term, make their old fossil-fuel business untenable. Rather than waiting for those pressures to build, wobbling the business, they got ahead of them. They saw the possibilities, not just the problems, then identified the areas where they already had the right competencies and that held the most potential – in Ørsted's case, wind energy – and doubled down. And they helped individual members of their teams to move with them in their new direction, retraining those working in coal-fired power plants to work instead on wind farms. Everyone at Ørsted was encouraged into the Mississippi mindset.

It's a mindset modelled brilliantly by the company's current CEO, Mads Nipper. He joined in 2020, and although he wasn't at the helm of the organization during its transformation, his own journey mirrors the bends in the river that Ørsted has seen and his leadership is now guiding the company on its gravitational route to the future.

A Solutionist through-and-through, Nipper understands that 'The straight line won't work,' and that, 'Realism is the determination to keep the pressure, and to know that sometimes we put that pressure here, sometimes we take a detour'.

Nipper proves that, just like with Ørsted itself, a change of heart – a new approach, a different perspective – can come later in your journey. After all, water stands still for years in Lake Itasca before making its way along the Mississippi's riverbed. Describing his earlier career at toy-company LEGO, Mads explains that 'for the first many years of my professional life, I thought I was selling toys and developing toys, then I realized I was not at all.' A full 15 years into his career, when he became Chief Marketing Officer of LEGO, he started to receive heartfelt letters from children and families, some with terminal illnesses or difficult circumstances, for whom playing with Lego brought joy and solace. 'If the product and the company I work for can make such a big difference in people's lives, in this case children's lives, this is much beyond a moulded plastic brick... So, it dawned on me that business is not just business. Business is a wonderful enabler to make a fantastic difference in the world and in people's lives.' It was a revelation that led him to engage differently with his career and ultimately to work for Ørsted, a place where he felt he could make the biggest positive impact on the world.

A Mississippi mind also depends on something that is common to all Solutionists: curiosity. Because to look at an issue or challenge with an interested, open mind is the best way to engage productively with it. As Nipper puts it, 'One of the things senior leaders too often stop doing is asking ourselves questions. We stop being curious, because we get so busy doing what we think is the best thing.'

Nipper asked questions and found his answers revealed part of himself that was steadfast, and that only his actions had to change: 'My fundamental values and especially how I treat other people – they have not changed.' He is clear that changing your course needn't mean changing yourself. In fact, firm foundations are an anchor for new ideas and different approaches: 'I'm, of course, determined to act if the financials or other operations are not good. But it doesn't change my motivation or determination or self-esteem or self-confidence, because I know that what we do is much beyond just that.'

It is unsurprising, then, that today, with their radical transformation almost complete, Ørsted continues under Nipper's leadership to adapt its thinking. Having established itself as an offshore wind company, it has now diversified its offering with onshore wind and solar energy. There are no straight lines here, only the flex and flow, bends and brilliance of solutionism.

Although, some bends might be sharper than others.

First, fall in love with failure

Many of the most successful Solutionists I know are remarkably fond of failure. By its very nature, doing something new and different, something better for people and planet, is difficult. Failure is baked into the process – indeed, it is the only way to find success.

So, while you obsess about your goals, you need to stay fluid and experimental with how you reach them. Hold your plans lightly and be ready for them to change. Which is to say, you should foster what is called an 'adaptive mindset' by psychologists. Adaptive thinking requires you to embrace what others shy away from – it welcomes change, is excited by new perspectives and sees setbacks as opportunities. As Kees Aarts of the insect-farming firm Protix puts it, 'Always champagne. In victory I deserve it, in defeat I need it. I can tell you I have a rule: every deal, no matter what the outcome is, we drink champagne.'

During what he affectionately calls 'the worm poop years', TerraCycle's founder, Tom Szaky, found a way to turn worm poop into fertilizer, which he packaged up in used plastic bottles. He was pleased to have uncovered a business model that could be both profitable and responsible – an approach that ran counter to an idea that had shocked Szaky in economics class, that the purpose of business is to only maximize profits for shareholders.

The year was 2001, and Szaky began operations from his dorm room at Princeton University. Within four months, he'd dropped out of school to run the business full-time. And within five years, his fertilizer was on the shelves of Target and Home Depot stores, and Szaky had built a headquarters in New Jersey made partly out of landfill-bound plastic – a problem bigger than worm poop.

Szaky was keenly aware of that problem with waste. He knew that only a small proportion of plastic ever got recycled, and that, simultaneously, demand for recycled plastic was much higher than supply.

So, he pivoted the company. TerraCycle turned its focus away from worms and towards the 30 per cent of items that end up in recycling bins, but aren't fit for standard recycling processes – think chocolate bar wrappers, baby food pouches and plastic forks. His goal was ending waste, and while his fertilizer solution worked, it didn't tackle the problem that made his mind itch. Now, he's pivoting again to Loop, the circular business. Tom is very open to the idea that his ideas might need to change.

Ørsted's Mads Nipper is also adamant about this:

> We need to do away with the fear of failure… We will make mistakes – I make mistakes every single day. If our mantra was, 'in order to save the world, the best way is to not make any mistakes', then this fear of failure, I guarantee you, would end in a smoking disaster for our grandchildren. Instead, we must have a boldness, the courage to make mistakes, and an acceptance that, 'yes, that didn't work, and that's fine because we learnt from it'.

Only the long-term view – the hallmark of a Solutionist's outlook – can see mistakes as the stepping-stones they are to much bigger future success.

Flex your mindset

Flexible or adaptive thinking is critical to what scientist Carol Dweck calls the 'power of yet'. In her research with schoolchildren, she found that when confronted with a written problem that was slightly too advanced for them to solve, the kids reacted in one of two ways.

Some felt they had failed catastrophically, that their intelligence had been judged and found wanting. This is what Dweck termed a 'fixed mindset'. Others responded quite differently, seeing the too-hard test as a challenge they could enjoy learning to overcome. They had a 'growth mindset': the ability, as Dweck puts it, to 'luxuriat[e] in the power of yet', instead of being 'gripped in the tyranny of now'. Not only do children with growth mindsets feel less distressed when they don't pass a test, they also perform better, over time, than those with fixed mindsets (Dweck, 2014).

Both success and sanity for Solutionists lie in cultivating this flexible mindset. After all, anyone can learn to be better at anything, including having a growth mindset. That's exactly the point.

Mads Nipper is a walking example of Dweck's 'growth mindset': seeing something difficult as an opportunity to overcome it. 'I always see the positive things in a situation,' he says. 'So, instead of saying, "we will never roll out renewable energy fast enough, because of all these barriers," I'm saying, "the technologies exist, the money is there, the organizations are there, and yes there are a few road-blocks we need to remove, but all the fundamentals are there."' This is the 'power of yet' in action. Nipper wields this flexibility of thought in conversation, particularly with those who don't agree with him. An opposing view is not a blocker for Nipper, but a chance to bring someone else on side. He explains that if, for example, a politician says climate change isn't their priority, he will ask what is. Perhaps they are more interested in job creation. 'Then what I would do,' Nipper explains, 'is I would say, "you know what, actually rolling out renewable energy at scale is a fantastic opportunity to create new, better, decent-paying jobs for people who will otherwise work in an industry where the jobs are going to disappear".' In this way, he says, 'I don't try to convince sceptics, I actually listen to them and then I come back with arguments that exactly address their priorities'. It is an innocent yet deft sleight of hand that can pull everyone onto the same – more sustainable – page.

How often do you feel like you're allowed to change your mind? It often feels like we are expected to follow through on our first idea, to stay the course – to avoid, at all costs, the possibility of being 'flaky' or 'giving up'.

When it comes to being a Solutionist, your success is dependent on your flexibility. Consider that sentence the permission you need to change your mind.

Don't sink your costs

A real struggle for Solutionists is when they find the wrong solution. It happens, and it doesn't mean you are any less of a Solutionist – just that you must keep trying.

It's so very hard to admit when our brilliant plan is showing signs of failure; it's not the answer we hoped for. There is a moment of realization, when the numbers don't stack up or the product won't quite work. Our hearts race in the same moment that our stomachs drop – what should I do next?

All too often, people repeat their failure a few more times (or for a few more years), expecting a different result, rather than flexing, reinventing, lateral designing and getting down the river another way.

The reason we cling onto projects, ideas and answers that no longer serve us is because humans carry a weird bias that many other animals don't: we commit the 'sunk-cost fallacy'. This is what happens when you sit down at the cinema to watch a film you've been desperate to see, but halfway through realize it's not all it's cracked up to be. You're bored, fidgety and thinking about what else you could be doing. You've come all the way here and paid for your ticket, so leaving now would be a waste, right? You sit it out until the credits roll. The reality is that doing so didn't get you your money back, and only cost you more wasted time.

It's difficult to let go of the idea of a sunk cost, but let go we must. Solutionists' worlds revolve around outcomes. This means looking, focused and unwavering, at the future, not the past. If plan A hasn't taken you closer to your outcome, drop it like a hot potato. The efforts and resources ploughed into it in recent weeks, months, years – that time resource should not dictate your decision to stick or twist. It belongs to yesterday, and your vision lives on the horizon of tomorrow.

As Bertrand Swiderski, Chief Sustainability Officer of giant French retailer Carrefour put it to me, 'We have to act and repeat concrete actions, to test and learn and act again.'

The faster you can act, learn and flex into plan B, the quicker you can save the world.

Let's get gritty

Even if many meanders don't quite work out, the Mississippi always gets there. Being flexible, learning to love failure and dodging the sunk-cost fallacy are bends in the curve of the river. What doesn't change is the relentless flow of water. While you are going to adapt to what you learn on the way, you're never going to stop moving towards your goal.

One of the questions I asked of my interviewees for this book was, 'If I could open a time tunnel back to a younger version of you, what would you shout down that tunnel before it collapsed?' Some of my favourite answers include 'don't dye your hair pink' and 'ask for more money, every time.' Many Solutionists hesitated, taking a long pause before answering. When I asked why, they explained that any advice they gave might change the course of their lives, and they wouldn't want to risk that. A glorious example of having no regrets when you live firmly aligned with your values.

The most common response, by far, was 'Just Keep Going!' Each of these Solutionists had hit moments where they'd adapted, they'd invented, they dodged and weaved to get their solution into reality, but it still wasn't working. Their solutions were right, but the market wasn't quite ready. Probably, millions of other people who were trying to get going also sat, dejected, on the very same day. What distinguished the Solutionists was that they didn't allow dejection to become defeat. Many people who have given up on their goals because the course meandered too much might have had brilliant ideas. Only those with tenacity made them happen.

That's why 'grit' is one of the five points on your star.

Irma Olguin Jr, the co-founder and CEO of Bitwise Industries, has a story with grit literally ground into it. I was mesmerized when she told it to me:

I grew up in a very small town, about 2,000 people, in the heart of central California where it's very hot and dry. You could pretty well divide my school by the kids of the folks who owned and managed land, and the kids of the families who worked on the land. I was in the latter group. My family had migrated to central California following the work, as so many Mexican families did. That's what I thought I would do with my life: the same thing that my family did, and my version of success was the ability to pay all of our bills in the same month. This was a place and time where it was completely normal to trade rent for groceries or your utilities bill for a car payment.

The divide in the community was apparent in a number of ways. You knew who was going to play soccer on the weekends, those were the children of the field labourers. You knew who was going to be on a travelling baseball team with the new equipment, those were the children of the folks who managed or owned the land, right? But as we got older another difference started to become apparent and that is that certain kids were planning their lives after high school, leaving town and going to college. And certain kids were thinking about which job they could get a hold of the quickest and whether or not community college might fit around it.

I was in the camp of maybe get some community college credits someday but absolutely getting a full-time job as soon as humanly possible. Then, when I was 15 years old I was sitting in a classroom and they announced that the PSAT (Preliminary Standardized Aptitude Test) was being held in the cafeteria. Not being college-bound, I didn't know what that meant but I was 15 years old and I did understand that I could get out of class for half a day. So, I ended up sitting for this test which would turn out to be where colleges get your details to send you information. College marketing material began arriving at my house and these were full colour, glossy, printed on heavy paper. Paraphrasing, they would say, 'Dear Irma, do you want to come to college?' That was a new thought for me, that in fact maybe I did want to go to college. But if you flip to the pricing page in any one of those catalogues, you know that's just not going to be a reality for some folks, and I was one of those folks. The mail kept arriving and I would read every single one. I opened every envelope, I flipped through every catalogue and began imagining myself as one of those kids with the backpacks on, walking across the courtyard of a college.

At one point, a letter arrived that was an offer for a full academic scholarship if I could prove that I had extracurriculars and provide my transcripts. So, I went down that path. To claim the scholarship, it was mandatory that you arrive at an orientation and that you check-in. I told my parents and they were really sad about it. That was a hard conversation. I remember them telling me I couldn't go because it was across the country and how would a person like me ever get there, right? So, I started to convince them to help me collect cans and bottles from the fields that we lived in so that I could recycle them for a few cents and buy a Greyhound bus ticket. We collected a lot of cans.

That was how I got from Fresno, California to Toledo, Ohio. The first thing I noticed though was that, even in the not-good side of town, I couldn't point to another brown person. Here I was across the country, 17 years old, with my duffel bag swung over my shoulder, and I didn't recognize anything around me. I go to orientation, and I tell them that I'm here to claim my scholarship, and the woman across the table is very welcoming, excited to have me, and she explained to me what a major was and how to choose one.

I noticed a beautiful glass building in the catalogue and I thought to myself, 'It would be really cool to take classes in a glass building.' So, I pointed to that, and she said, 'That's the college of engineering.' I said, 'Okay, then I think my major is engineering,' which is how I ended up in computer science and computer engineering. It was one of those happy accidents that would change my existence. I ended up working as an engineer – still the only Latina, queer person from California that I could see for miles and miles around, no network, no real skills to speak of, bottom of the totem pole, but I was out-earning everybody I knew at home. I knew that in this industry, if I did all the right things, worked hard and didn't let anybody know that I didn't belong here, then I was going to be rich. And that's what happened. By the third or fourth cheque that came into my pocket I was paying all of my bills in the same month, I was ordering anything I wanted off the menu. Things were changing for me and I thought, this is what it feels like to be rich and to not be terrified all the time.

Eventually, there was one moment where my colleagues and I were working late and we ordered a pizza and my colleague comes to me, grabs the cash, he's going to pay the delivery guy. My colleague calls back to me, 'Hey Irma, how much do you want to leave for a tip?' And I yell back to my colleague, 'Tell him to keep the change.' Nobody knew this was happening, but my whole existence was flipped on its head in that moment because I'd never not counted the change. So, that's one of the most defining moments for me that I knew I needed to reorient my life not just around finding my success story but then being able to contribute to other people's success stories. Fast forward a few years, that's what Bitwise Industries tries to replicate, the technology education that changed my life, the glass building that we call castles for underdogs, the job itself that creates more of those keep-the-change moments. I get to dedicate myself to trying to recreate that again and again and again for people who either look like me or grew up in a similar way, and what could be more motivating than that?

Irma's story of grit is stunning, and she's made sure it's not unique. The average student who starts the Bitwise training programme makes less than $20,000 a year, and leaves with a job that earns them more than $60,000 a year.

Alongside skilling up under-represented groups, Bitwise wants to see space in the city used differently. First, they raised half a million dollars to buy a huge disused car dealership, which they transformed into Bitwise South

Stadium: a building with three floors of office space, a coffee shop and a 200-seat theatre. They went on to buy another 200,000 square feet of building space in downtown Fresno, which they have transformed into lively office, retail and restaurant space.

Bitwise has enabled the people of Fresno, whatever their background, to find decent work and be part of a thriving hub of activity and community. And in 2018, they were ready to find new cities to transform. They took their model to other 'underestimated' cities, starting with Bakersfield, Merced and Oakland in California. Their success has led them, in 2022, to roll out the same approach in cities in Ohio, New York, Texas, Colorado, New Mexico and Wyoming. Their work isn't only good news for the people they serve – it also makes business sense. By 2021, the company had secured $100 million in investments and is estimated to have taken $40 million in annual revenue. True grit, indeed.

Calculated grit

Angela Duckworth is a renowned psychologist whose research has uncovered two fascinating truths about this magical tenacity.

First, tenacity often predicts success more reliably than talent or IQ; and second, that anyone, adult or child, can learn to be gritty. These two revelations are great news for all Solutionists. Hard work beats natural talent and grit can be grown.

Honestly, that's always been my experience. I was no prodigy at school and, dragged down by dyslexia, my grades struggled to reach E for attainment. So, I worked my guts out to get A for effort every time. My mother assured me that, eventually, those effort grades would drag up my attainment. Years and years went by, with teachers praising how hard I worked while politely managing my expectations that vocational college might be too ambitious for me, let alone university. My mum's words reverberated around my head every semester of more disappointing results – effort will drag up attainment. Finally, to both my mum's and my great relief, it turned out she was right. I trotted off to university and then threw in a couple of Master's degrees, just because I could.

Just like all parts of the Mississippi mindset, grit can be grown:

1 You gotta love what you do – sometimes we need grit to survive, to make it through hard times, to feed the family even though you're too dog-tired to stand. That's a grit which I've known, and that people are waking up to every day. I salute them for it. There's another grit though, and one that I see in Solutionists when they work with and hold onto their vision for the sheer fun of it! Being excited by, enjoying working on, and finding joy in our solution is the very best way to never be defeated. That's why fun balances grit on opposite sides of the star.

2 Cut out the crap – my kryptonite is spending hours doom-scrolling on social media. I can burn through

hours, or days, surfing the latest outraged gossip on Twitter. That's not self-care, or joyful action, or even rest. It's crap, like sugar for the brain. It's easier to grit down and get on with solutions stuff when you're not distracted by the other waste-of-time stuff.

3 Find a tenacious tribe – isn't it always easier working hard when others around you are doing the same? And near impossible to buckle down surrounded by folks who are kicking back and want to chat? Tenacity is surprisingly infectious for something we too often consider an inner virtue. I've written this book in libraries, Futerra's offices, and in those cafés where everyone is pounding away at their keyboard. And in my day-job, I'm surrounded by some of the hardest-working, most dedicated and tenacious people I know. Grit loves good company.

4 Practise – grit is a muscle. When you first practise not giving up, it will open a deep well within you that perhaps you hadn't noticed was there. The more times you're about to sigh and stop, but instead sigh and keep going, the stronger that muscle will grow.

5 Forgive yourself – you're not a machine and sometimes when you buckle down to work your knees are just gonna buckle! Tenacity takes breaks, and if you don't take enough of them your head and body are going to schedule them in without telling you. This section on hard-working, resolute and gritty determination is written in the same book with a chapter on joy and rest. Because if today isn't a tenacious day – forgive yourself.

The co-founders of Social Supermarket met as rowers in college. Jamie Palmer, the CEO, laughed making the comparison, 'Knowing each other from rowing meant we already had a common interest in putting ourselves through a lot of long hours and misery to reach a common goal. Rowing is a lot of blood, sweat and tears, just like a start-up.' What they learnt is that many other students really wanted to win and become top rowers, but then only turned up for rowing practice twice a week. Winning required frosty mornings out on the river, arms aching and head wondering why it wasn't back on its warm pillow – 10 times a week. When I asked Jamie who had given him advice that has stayed with him as a successful entrepreneur, it was his rowing coach of years ago. The coach told the winning team every week, 'It's not how much you want it, it's how much you're willing to work for it that matters.'

Eyes on the horizon

The final part of the Mississippi mind is to cling onto your long-term vision amid all the noisy distractions of short-term action. Of course, this is a key principle of sustainable business itself.

I've had the pleasure of working with Daniel Servitje Montull, the CEO of the world's biggest baker, Grupo Bimbo. Readers based in Spanish speaking communities across the world likely grew up with household-name Bimbo products in their kitchens and lunchboxes. If you did, I'm pleased to tell you that Grupo Bimbo has committed to huge new goals on regenerative agriculture, renewable energy and serving a healthy 'planetary' diet. When I asked Daniel how the company has achieved such ambition, he explained the power of long-term thinking:

> I have been blessed in my career, that Grupo Bimbo has always maintained a very long perspective on things. To me, this is a big difference in this company versus others, that you are allowed the luxury of thinking on what's good for the company over time, not just today. Many of our sustainability initiatives, if we looked at them just with the common short-term view that many businesses have, we simply wouldn't have been able to do them. To me, that's killing many of the big solutions of the world. So, our competitive advantage is to invest in long-term solutions, and then harvest those rewards.

His colleague, and a great friend of mine, Rafael Pamias Romero, was even blunter when talking about the dangers of quarterly financial reporting which traps companies into needing to demonstrate returns on any investment in just three months. He states, 'Quarters are cancer'.

I couldn't agree more. Solutions rarely come quickly, and the bigger the potential the longer those huge rewards will take to realize. Every single Solutionist I have spoken to, worked alongside and surveyed has a long-term heart and short-term hands. They are tenacious and bold in the choices they make, and swiftly adapt to boulders in their path, because they cleave only to their purpose, not to any particular project, product or process.

Ezgi Barcenas, Chief Sustainability Officer at AB InBev, explains how that works in practice. 'I don't shy away from rolling up my sleeves. What we do is not just about being hopeful and positive about the future, it's actually urgently working towards that positive future that you believe in. Ask yourself "if not me, who?" If there's a problem, let's just dig in and solve it.'

In the end, all of the twists and tumbles, flows and fights of the river are simply a means for the water to reach the vastness of the ocean – its home.

EXERCISE   Solutions starters

1   Articulate the vision point of your star as a mission statement or a motto.

2   Being too prescriptive, e.g. 'We'll turn over a billion and save a gigatonne of carbon', is a laudable target, but a true vision has emotional flare and poetry to it. Futerra's mission is to 'Make The Anthropocene Awesome' and I challenge you to create one as weird, memorable and compelling as that.

3   Keep a 'school fees' tally. That's the term which Karen, Futerra's CFO, uses for what we've learnt through every failure. Solutionists are notoriously bad at reflection; because their heads are so firmly facing forward, they can struggle to look back at what's come before. Keeping a record of what didn't work, why and what you've learnt has a wonderful ability to reduce your likelihood of making the same mistake again.

4   Try the 9-minute rule. When you just want to give up, or can't even get started, set a phone timer for 9 minutes.

Then work, diligently and without distraction, for those 9 minutes. That's long enough to solve a little problem, get mentally engaged in a project or overcome your fear of starting. You can stop after the 9 minutes… but you might not want to.

5 Bill Gates reminds us, 'We always overestimate the change that will occur in the next two years and underestimate the change that will occur in the next ten'. If your vision is only for the next quarter, or business cycle, you might be disappointed by what you can get done. Dedicate a decade to something? Your impact will be sensational.

CHAPTER FIVE

Fix it formula

In a landing dock off the coast of Maine, USA, a fishing boat pulls up and bobs on the water. It's loaded with bulging sacks of shining green-brown tendrils: seaweed. More specifically, kelp. Driving the boat is a former lobster-man, who had, until recently, focused all his efforts on catching the lobsters that Maine is famous for, and which were the bedrock of the state's economy.

Then, warming waters because of climate change meant that Maine's lobster population moved along the coast and further offshore. With numbers dropping, lobstering fami-lies faced an uncertain future. Meanwhile, the same chang-ing temperatures has caused other species to move into the area. This includes the endangered North Atlantic right whale, which can get tangled up in lobster pots and nets.

The answer to these economic, social and environmental woes is waving fronds. Like all plants, kelp absorbs carbon while giving off oxygen. It can be grown without fertilizer and even benefits the health of nearby mussels, which clean the water around them. It's also a tasty, nutrient-dense food that can be used in anything from salads to plant-based burgers. It plugged the gap left by a faltering local industry, while providing healthy food and supporting the coastal ecosystem.

Economic, social and environmental benefits all rolled into one. This is the sweet-spot formula Solutionists are looking for. It's what I call 'full-stack' solutions.

Fill your stack

The phrase comes from computer science. Software developers layer up different pieces of software to produce a 'full-stack' solution that will work in our complex online world. Even the most basic website tends to have a solution stack of operating system, middleware, database and applications. The best digital experts are called 'full-stack' developers because they can build in all the component parts of a functional website, from the friendly user experience to the complex back-end of programming language.

This is an excellent metaphor for the modern Solutionist. Rather than just specializing in one part of our solutions stack, say solar energy, we need to become masters of the entire stack, of solar energy, equitable energy access, non-exploitative mineral mining, climate justice and end-use recycling of the panels. Our solutions must consider not just the original answer that we thought up, but our product, service or business model's full impact on society (or environment if your solution is social). There's no point creating a commercially viable solution for girls' education that has such a negative impact on the environment that it endangers those very girls' futures. A new sustainable material that can radically cut waste isn't truly a solution if manufacturing or harvesting that material exploits workers.

Full-stack Solutionists understand that every answer needs to be intersectional. Thankfully, we know that with a little thought, full-stack solutions can serve climate justice, intersectional environmentalism, equity and just transitions – all at once.

We know because the IPCC checked whether climate solutions are good for society (when well implemented). They reviewed the whole array of 'demand-side' solutions – from changing buildings, to travel, to agriculture – to find the changes that carry the biggest carbon savings. Their conclusion? That by 2050, if we deploy these solutions at full scale, we could save up to 70 per cent more end-use carbon than business-as-usual scenarios (2022). The IPCC doesn't get out of bed for less than a gigatonne of carbon, so they are telling us a solutions revolution can defeat the climate monster. They also dug into mountains of evidence about whether these changes will make our lives better, or worse. In the rather dry language of climate science, they conclude they have 'high confidence' that these solutions are 'consistent with improving basic wellbeing for all'.

The 'for all' bit of that statement is a very big deal. They calculated that 'decent living standards' – what humans need for wellbeing – for everyone are 'achievable through the implementation of high-efficiency low demand mitigation pathways'.

People agree. When Futerra surveyed folk in the UK and the United States about sustainable actions they could take at home, like eating less meat and travelling by bike, we asked if those sustainable lifestyle changes would improve or worsen their quality of life. Over half of those who took part on both sides of the Atlantic thought big changes to how they eat, travel and buy would improve their life, and only 11 per cent were worried they might worsen it.

This is the solutions stack: solving climate change and improving wellbeing all in a socially just way. Full-stack Solutionists develop end-to-end answers across everything.

Multiply your wins

Throughout this book, you've heard me describe the wonderful win–wins of solutions. The best business ideas solve real problems, and doing so usually makes huge financial sense. Truly sustainable products attract like-minded customers, whose loyalty fuels your bottom line.

More often than not, the wins needn't stop there. The thing about tackling the world's biggest problems is that none exists in isolation. The mess that our planet finds itself in is the product of systemic problems that run deep. When acidifying oceans disrupt underwater ecosystems, they also affect fishing communities' livelihoods. When clothes are mass produced with toxic dyes, habitats suffer, workers are harmed and the world's supply of safe drinking water is undermined. The same air pollution that leads to unpredictable weather patterns also damages the health of children's lungs.

We have long recognized that different issues intersect, and the concept of environmental justice – which sees human rights and equality as integral to environmental issues, and vice versa – is finally entering the mainstream. We are becoming better able to see how habitat health and human health are one and the same, and to acknowledge the part that racism plays in people's experiences of the worst effects of climate change.

Not only do the problems interlink, so too do the solutions. Address one issue and another is solved with it. Reduce our carbon emissions to stop the oceans acidifying, and marine life can thrive along with fishing communities' income. Banish toxic fabric dyes and the fish surrounding a factory benefit, along with the factory's employees and those who rely on the local water supply. Reduce gas-guzzling car fumes to slow down extreme weather while also protecting kids' health. (If I were less fond of the natural world, I'd probably be mentioning something about killing two – or three, or ten – birds with one stone.)

There's every chance that with the right approach, your solution could have many facets – it could be a gem that reflects light on a glittering array of human and planetary health. And when it does, my goodness, it's beautiful to behold.

Nice bum

That's one of the slogans plastered on the box of Who Gives A Crap, a sustainably made toilet paper, where 50 per cent of the company's profits go towards building toilets in places that need them.

Danny Alexander, one of the founders of the business, told me that 40 per cent of the world's population doesn't have access to a toilet, meaning that one child dies every two minutes from diseases caused by poor water and sanitation. That's the problem that made him itch: 'Our 30-year goal as a business is to ensure every single person on Earth has access to clean water and a toilet by the year 2050.'

He and his two co-founders released their first product in 2013. The packaging comes in bright colours and zany patterns, and the brand doesn't shy away from a toilet joke or two. They have achieved what only the best sustainable brands have done: they've made doing good feel fun. And, while most standard toilet paper is made from trees, often to the detriment of some of the world's most important forests, Who Gives A Crap's is made instead from bamboo or recycled paper.

Environmentally friendly, building toilets where they are needed, with fun consumer benefits thrown in. It's a full-stack solution, but a demanding one from a financial perspective.

Most businesses with large ambitions for scale go through a period early on of loss-making. That wasn't an option for us. We couldn't go to our customers in the early years and say, thanks for supporting us, we donated zero dollars this year. We had to be high growth but also maintain profitability to meet our donation targets, so it was incredibly challenging. However, that gave us tremendous discipline. We knew the value of every dollar we were spending and everything that we were doing.

By 2017, Who Gives A Crap had donated more than a million dollars towards building toilets. And when the pandemic sent shoppers into a toilet-paper-buying frenzy, sales reached dizzying heights. In February 2020, sales doubled overnight, then reached 40 times their usual rate just four days later. At their peak, they were selling 28 rolls every second. In 2020 alone they donated $5.9 million to charity. Danny didn't flinch from the 50 per cent of profit commitment: 'I feel 100 per cent confident that promise has been a driver of our growth, and it is one of the strongest reasons why we're successful today. Although it's difficult, I would argue it's essential for a business like ours.'

By 2021, the company had customers in 40 countries, and had raised $41.5 million from a range of high-profile investors on the start-up scene. However big they grow, Who Gives A Crap are determined to stay, as they put it, 'true to their roots: toilet humour and making the world a better place'.

For Danny, building a full-stack solution has become self-reinforcing:

> Ninety-nine per cent of what we do as a business is tweaking an ad for Facebook, or adjusting the size of a box, or making a fun email to send people, or making a ridiculous video teaching people how to make crafts with our wrappers. But, I make sure our people have a sense of how those small tasks ladder up to that big 30-year goal, so they don't have

to actively think about the problem when they're doing the daily work. That's one huge benefit of our business model: we're in the solution space and we don't have to dwell very much in the problem space.

This is full-stack-solving, and it can radically accelerate our progress towards an all-round brighter, safer, healthier, happier, more diverse and abundant world.

Start stacking

On first look, the early days of your solution – your gem – might look unpolished. Hold it up to the light: are there angles you'd not seen before? Are there more facets you can polish into existence?

There are ways you can begin to multiply your solution.

1. Zoom out

A singular solution slots neatly into one space – the environment, say, or workers' rights. Given what we know about how issues intersect, keeping any problem or solution in one box is unnecessarily limiting. The trick is to take a step back. Zoom out, and look for the dotted lines that span across the scene in front of you. Where do they join up?

Majora Carter applied just this kind of thinking to the area in which she grew up. She has worked to transform a fading area of the Bronx, New York, which suffered economic and social degradation after white families left the area in the 1970s. The people of colour who remained in the neighbourhood were left to suffer the consequences of less investment and more pollution. Carter was determined to bring in resources, to make the Bronx feel thriving and liveable again. She secured grant money to create a riverside community park, and went on to spearhead initiatives to clean up the shores of the Bronx River and offer urban-green-collar training programmes that would involve local people in the environment and other issues related to living in the Bronx.

She could see something that others maybe didn't spot: the point at which the need for decent jobs, clean air and human connection intersect. Namely, the need for safe, accessible real estate.

As Majora put it to me, 'In the States, there's a reason why there's this huge wealth gap and if we think about the lower end of the wealth gap – who's most affected by climate issues? Who's most affected by health issues, education? It has to do with real estate. And I'm like, "So why are we not talking about that?"' Rather than see the problem of pollution and focus only on environmental initiatives, she saw it nestled among other social needs and challenges. The result has been a solution that reaches right across, and deep within, an entire ecosystem of human and non-human lives.

2. Bust silos

The Espigoladors in Spain collect fruit and veg that farmers don't want because they are surplus or imperfectly shaped. Volunteers gather the food, and most of it is given to people who might not otherwise have access to nutritious food – to the tune of nearly 7 million portions, at the time of writing. That's the philanthropic bit. They turn the rest into jams and preserves, sell them at a healthy premium and create jobs for people at risk of social exclusion. Tackling hunger, providing jobs, and preventing the environmental harms of food waste, all in one fell swoop.

Once we observe how social and environmental issues relate to each other, the lines we usually draw around them begin to fall away. Where there were silos – biodiversity, climate, health, human rights – there's something that looks more like a web. Seeing it this way makes it easier to break down the walls we have constructed between different areas.

3. A little more conversation

The more people involved in your idea, the more dots you can join. Full-stack-solving requires multiple skills, perspectives, talents and expertise. As we have seen, all are relevant – from the health policy wonk to the women's rights activist, the creative communicator to the carbon capture entrepreneur.

It's crucial that we also don't forget everyday citizens, community members, and those most often overlooked. Seek out those adjacent to your idea – people who live near your factory, perhaps, or already work in an industry you're trying to change. Make it easy for them to take part in the conversation, bearing in mind this could involve offering childcare, grants or transportation. Seek out the stories of those facing the reality of so many of the world's crises, and let them be your guide. They can help you honestly and thoroughly interrogate the question of whom your project really benefits, and identify any knock-on effects – like gentrification, job losses or impacts on cultural traditions – that you might otherwise overlook.

As Leah Penniman, the founder of Soul Fire Farm, told me, 'Those most impacted by climate change globally and regionally are the ones who have the solutions. Black and brown communities, displaced communities, poor communities, farmers, peasants, people who work the land, need to be in leadership and headed, not tokenized or ignored and certainly not left to deal with the consequences of the actions of the wealthy nations.'

Your goal here is to multiply the number of voices involved in your solution – and to really, thoughtfully listen.

4. Pain = Gain

Looking at one problem is hard; looking at many is harder. Philosophers and scientists have long understood that the human brain prefers the simple over the complicated. In the 14th century, William of Occam came up with Occam's Razor: the concept that the simplest idea is always the preferable one. Today's cognitive scientists have gone on to establish this bias in practice.

Given our need for simplicity, the dot-joining, complexity-embracing world of full-stack-solving isn't our brains' idea of fun. In the planning stages, multi-solving might feel daunting, overwhelming – painful even. Finding the right collaborators, blending viewpoints, listening to others, learning constantly – these are all challenging but necessary parts of shifting into multi-solutionism. So be ready to bolster your resilience (check out Chapter 10 on joyful entrepreneurship for tips) and remember that, once you move into action, your solutions will allow you to put a big, satisfying tick in many boxes at once. Your extra upfront effort will make an exponentially bigger impact.

5. Embrace experimentation

When solutions sprawl into many spheres, you can't be expected to map them accurately. You can consult, plan and strategize your first few steps, but you can't know all the unknowns. And you wouldn't want to: these are where chance encounters, accidental triumphs and unexpected inspiration happen. Leave space for them – while being sure to document your successes and failures, big and small.

Sandrine Dixson-Declève is President of the Club of Rome and co-author of the groundbreaking Earth4All report. She says, 'We can't afford separate conversations and siloed policy on climate, biodiversity, inequality or poverty. What the world needs at this time of multiple crises is nothing less than five extraordinary 'turnarounds': ending poverty, addressing inequality, reaching gender equity, transitioning to clean energy and making our food system healthy for people and planet.'

That's the full-stack To-Do List for Solutionists, and the next chapter will help you plan how to do it.

EXERCISE   Solutions starters

Most of this chapter is a 'how to' on full-stack-solving. How can you make a start?

1   In the last box, I asked you to write up a mission or goals – take a look at them. What benefit do they bring the world?

---

2   Categorize those benefits as social, environmental, health, economic or others you can see.

3   Perhaps you have one or two categorized as 'environmental'. For each of these, ask: 'How can my work towards this goal create other benefits – health, community or equity?'

4   Do the same for goals and initiatives that currently exist in social categories – what benefits could they bring to local wildlife, carbon reduction or limiting water use? It follows that the goals and initiatives that deserve most of your attention are those that offer the longest list of full-stack benefits.

CHAPTER SIX

Hope is a business plan

Vision, grit, flexibility, fun and soul are the ingredients from which Solutionists emerge. This chapter will help you find the solution you'll serve with that star.

As you read through the following triggers, work out your stack. This is a chapter you can jump around in, looking for issues and topics that make you 'itch'. Extra points for answers that solve more than one of these challenges at once.

Are you the Solutionist who will crack…

1. The business of energy solutions

When we think about solving climate change, we usually think first of statuesque wind turbines, glinting solar panels, cosy geothermal pumps and even harvesting energy from the waves or food waste. So we should. For the world to be net zero by 2050 – the last bell at the survivable climate saloon – we must entirely transition to renewables.

Even a few years ago that felt terrifyingly unlikely. Today, renewables already provide almost a third of the world's electricity (IRENA, 2019). What changed? Solutionists like you committed their businesses (large and small) to buying 100 per cent renewables, which spurred financial Solutionists to invest, government Solutionist subsidies that underwrote innovation and inventive Solutionists to create cheaper, more powerful, and easier to install renewables.

The cost to generate one 'watt' of renewable energy fell by 80 per cent (IRENA, 2017), making most renewables cheaper than fossil fuels.

However, we've still got two-thirds of the way to go, or even further, because we don't just want to replace the energy we currently use, we want more, more, more. As we electrify transport with EVs and rail, we'll need more energy. As we bring the billion people without access to modern energy into the light, we'll need more energy. All the rest of our solutions, from education to health, will need to be powered by renewables if they are going to be truly full-stack.

It's the kind of global transformation that Solutionists were born for. If you're not already itching to get started, ask yourself:

- Can you make faster, smarter, cheaper renewables?
- There are a billion potential customers waiting for energy access. Is that your market?

- Will you be the one to crack renewable energy storage?
- Energy efficiency saves money and the planet. Will you be the first energy efficiency billionaire?

Need a little more motivation? According to the rather staid and conservative International Energy Association, 'Renewables are set to remain the number one power sector category for investment in 2022, after a record year in 2021 when more than $440 billion was spent for the first time ever' (IEA, 2022). This is a huge amount of capital flowing into energy solutions: 'Renewables, grids and storage now account for more than 80% of total power sector investment.' In one of their likely scenarios for 2030, the IEA sees annual spending on renewables as four times higher than today.

Hope as a business plan, indeed.

2. The business of infrastructure solutions

Office blocks and bridges, schools and subways, highways, houses and hospitals: all put an enormous burden on the environment both to build and to run. Buildings are responsible for 30–40 per cent of the emissions in today's cities, and that needs to be reduced by up to 90 per cent if we are to reach the 2050 emissions targets set at COP21 (C40, 2018).

Recent global analysis shows that in 2020, building emissions were 10 per cent lower than in 2015 – but that this was due to the economic slowdown and other behavioural changes that resulted from lockdowns (GABC,

2021). With huge growth projected in the building sector, particularly in Asia and Africa, decarbonization efforts need to redouble if we are to keep infrastructure from driving us further into the climate crisis.

Any organization that plans, builds or even works in a building – so, most organizations – have a role to play in making our infrastructure fit for the future.

So, what could the future of buildings look like? Here are just a few of the infrastructure solutions that feel like wide-open opportunities.

Physical, meet digital

Digitizing homes and hotels, malls and museums might sound space-age, but the technology is already here. Cloud-based tools exist that give engineers, architects and planners the information they need to reduce a structure's carbon footprint. Internet of Things (IoT) devices, like sensors and software, can detect, analyse and automatically adjust anything from lighting to humidity. And modelling technology can simulate different weather conditions and test buildings' climate resilience and how temperatures will affect living conditions. Despite this, the construction industry lags behind almost every other industry when it comes to digital transformation. It's time to catch up.

A system of systems

Imagine any piece of infrastructure – your local train station, say, or primary school. Whatever building you're picturing, it doesn't exist in a vacuum. Complicated as it might be to build and run, it is just one part of even more complex systems of people, transport and ecology. Cars, pedestrians, local residents, workers, wildlife and even weather all impact, and are impacted by, the infrastructure we humans build. How will your building affect the communities and ecology that surround it – and how could you make your impact a positive one? Biophilic design offers many solutions here, with buildings that integrate nature through green roofs, woodland creation, and designs that imitate natural patterns. They can capture rainwater, attract wildlife and reduce inhabitants' stress levels. From an economic perspective, the implications of this are nothing short of extraordinary: biophilic buildings result in employees taking less sick leave from offices, patients spending less time in hospitals, shoppers spending more in stores, students learning better in schools and less crime happening in communities.

Get retro(fitting)

Infrastructure solutions aren't just about building brand-new, more efficient buildings and facilities. Indeed, in some parts of the world, like Europe, four out of every five buildings that will exist in 2050 have already been built (McKinsey, 2021). As anyone who's lived in a 100-year-old house or flat will tell you, older buildings are often draughty and costly to maintain. We need to adapt what we have, to reimagine it for a decarbonized future. This is called retrofitting, and it could involve anything from better insulation to dimmable lights, improved ventilation and smart meters. Retrofitting is already a sizeable market, valued at $142.88 billion in 2020 – and only set to grow as new carbon reduction regulations are introduced (GVR, 2020).

These sorts of changes will lower energy bills, create jobs and improve people's health: yet another sustainability win–win–win:

- Smart buildings are the future, are you the Solutionist for it?
- Can you make the massive market for retrofit greener?
- What's your business plan for low-income property ownership?

The construction industry may not have kept up with others in the green transition, but it's set to move fast. It is estimated that there will be more than four billion connected IoT devices in commercial smart buildings by 2028 (Gartner, 2019). And 29 cities and 137 organizations have signed the World Green Building Council's Net Zero Carbon Buildings Commitment, pledging to meaningfully reduce carbon emissions in their buildings by 2030 (WGBC, 2022). Change is underway, and there's much more to be done. Now is the perfect time to jump on this big, green bandwagon.

3. The business of transport solutions

Getting from A to B is a carbon-heavy business. The transport sector accounts for 16 per cent of CO_2 emissions and is only set to pump out more (Ritchie, Roser and Rosado, 2020).

To achieve net zero by 2050, we need to see emissions from transport drop 20 per cent by 2050. With nearly 8 billion of us traversing the planet – some of us travelling further, faster and in a much more carbon-costly way than others – we need solutions, and fast.

How do we do it? The possible solutions are as many and varied as the journeys there are to be taken. Here are just three areas that are ready to be taken advantage of, with some examples to inspire your big idea.

Go public

Public transport is no longer seen as the clunky, dated inconvenience it once was. Notions of bleak buses and slow, stuffy old trains belong to generations gone by; Gen Z are turning to these options more readily than even their grandparents. A US study has shown that public transport makes up 31 per cent of Gen Z's journeys, compared with 25 per cent for Gen X and older (Movin'On, 2021). This isn't to say that Gen Z don't expect more from public transport: they're looking for more comfort, better connections with other modes of transport, and lower prices. Could you give it to them?

Innovations are already making public transport options preferable to gas-guzzling cars. Bus Rapid Transit (BRT) is a system that has made its way to cities around the world, and is designed to make buses fast, comfortable and cost-effective. The original BRT was set up in Curitiba, Brazil. When architect Jaime Lerner took office as mayor in 1971, he transformed the city in ways only a visionary architect could. Perhaps his greatest stroke of genius was the bus network, which he designed to resemble a train system. Dedicated bus lanes zipped passengers around the city via new bus stations on roads' central reservation. Paying before boarding further speeded things up, as did multiple doors for boarding. Despite journey speeds being comparable to a train network, the first rapid bus lanes of Curitiba ended up costing 50 times less than rail. Within a couple of decades Curitiba's nifty bus networks were carrying 1.5 million passengers every day (Reed, 2015).

Other cities the world over have gone on to adopt the BRT in evolving forms. A clever solution introduced more recently is called 'Transit Signal Priority', which, simply put, makes bus journeys quicker (hurrah!) by using sensors at traffic lights to make sure buses get through the lights quicker. Less time spent in traffic is a sure-fire way to make taking the bus more attractive than driving.

Two legs and two wheels

Encouraging walking and cycling is the most obvious way to cut the emissions of any journey to zero. For more people to choose to people power's transport it needs to be not only feasible for their journey but convenient, safe and enjoyable. How can we tempt more people to power themselves?

Here's one idea. In an ingenious move from the most bike-friendly country in the world, the city of Odense in Denmark has introduced traffic-light sensors that detect when it's raining and a cyclist is approaching, so it can offer a longer green light. Less time getting soaked means more people out and about on two wheels.

A short train ride east to Copenhagen, and cycle super-highways have had a measurable impact on people's willingness to take to two wheels. These wide, straight cycle paths cross roads as little as possible, and connect 30 municipalities surrounding the city. The result has been a 23 per cent increase in cyclists, with 14 per cent of these new cyclists previously having travelled by car. And the health benefits alone of cycle superhighways led to a socio-economic surplus of €616 million (Adams, 2019).

Boosting walkability is equally important. Pedestrianized areas, safe, well-lit sidewalks, smaller blocks, shaded paths and plentiful benches all make cities easier and more enjoyable to get around on foot. Living in a walkable neighbourhood has been found to be associated with lower rates of obesity and diabetes (Creatore et al, 2016), and could save travellers nearly $4 trillion in car operating costs by 2050 (Project Drawdown, 2020).

Get futuristic

Cars as we know them, data suggests, are on the out. Research shows that since the 1980s, the number of 17-year-olds getting their driver's licence has almost halved. Millennials are driving less than the generations that came before them, and Gen Z are buying even fewer cars than Millennials did at their age (Sivak and Schoettle, 2016). Those Gen Zers who do want to buy their own wheels are set on going electric, with 36 per cent saying their next car will be an electric vehicle (EV) compared to just 16 per cent of Gen X. Anything that can make EV life more convenient and fun will chime with this growing market of EV fans.

We have already seen Millennials and Gen Z drive the use of ride-hailing apps like Lyft and Uber – in the United States, 16–34-year-olds reportedly make up as much as two-thirds of Uber's user base (GWI, 2017). Their adventurous transport spirit doesn't end with smartphone-booked cabs. Gen Z in particular are keener than their older counterparts on alternative forms of transport like e-scooters and e-bikes. There's a world of decarbonized, sharing-economy transport waiting to be built. The likes of Lime and Bird (described by one of its investors as possibly being 'the fastest-growing company ever') (Yakowicz, 2019) are leading the way, but this is just the beginning. A new generation of travellers are ready for more. So, get your e-skates on.

Smartphones also mean physically travelling from place to place is less necessary. Why face traffic when you can get food delivered to your door, while you FaceTime a friend and browse for a new outfit online? The vehicle of the future might be none at all. How can you make everyday experiences like working, chatting, gaming, eating and watching as fulfilling and sociable from home as it can be elsewhere?

Of course, we can't talk about green transport without talking about the Dumbo-in-the-room: planes. Aviation is responsible for 2.5 per cent of all global CO_2 emissions (Ritchie, 2020) and, shockingly, some analysis shows that taking even a single short-haul flight generates more carbon emissions than the average person in some countries around the world produces in a whole year (Kommenda, 2019). It's an industry that's crying out for disruption, and it's looking like the future could include electric- and hydrogen-powered planes, cleverly redesigned wings and cabins, and smart route mapping. Not to mention airships, which could cut emissions from short-haul flights by up to 90 per cent (Neate, 2021).

Sea, land or air, the world needs no end of new ideas and creative thinking to drive us into a new era of green transport. Consider:

- Can you make teleworking popular, sane and lucrative?
- How could you sell walking and cycling solutions in heavily metropolitan areas?
- Public transport is ripe for a Gen Z led boom. Will you lead the way?
- Can you think laterally about affordable EVs?
- Airships are ready to take to the skies – could you give them lift-off?

New transport solutions are nothing short of a money spinner. In an analysis conducted by the Stockholm Environmental Institute for the Coalition for Urban Transitions, a plan to develop clean, connected, compact cities is estimated to yield as much as US$24 trillion over the next 30 years (Coalition for Urban Transitions, 2019). The analysis shows that the returns on shifting to low-carbon transport are far greater than those of other sectors. What are you waiting for?

4. The business of food solutions

For many lucky folk, food is one of life's great pleasures. For others it is a daily challenge to find enough to eat, and getting harder. The world's farmers grow an incredible

4 billion tonnes of food every year (Gustavsson et al, 2011). Enough, technically, to feed everyone. And yet over one person in ten goes hungry each day (FAO, 2022b, p 3).

Meanwhile, the corn and cows, milk and melons we produce are ravaging our resources. Food production is responsible for 37 per cent of all greenhouse gas emissions (Xu et al, 2021), and is degrading the soil it relies on at a rate of 24 billion tonnes a year (UNCCD, 2017, p 52).

The problems here are about as urgent as it gets. Here's some solution-flavoured food for thought.

Land's end

Incredibly, a whole half of the world's habitable land is used to grow food (Ritchie, 2019). And while scenes of rolling green fields and golden crops have come to be associated with rural idyll, they are in fact emblematic of ecological disaster. When vast swathes of land are populated by a single crop, no other life can thrive. Wildlife is forced to find other areas to grow, nest and feed; most of it is lost altogether. Of the species at risk of extinction today, agriculture is the threat to 86 per cent of them (Benton et al, 2021). Our farming practices also account for a horrifying 80 per cent of deforestation (FAO, 2022a, p 47).

Clear-cutting land for farming also has disastrous consequences for those who live on it. Indigenous communities are forced to protect their land; many lose it. And communities living near industrial farming facilities around the world face air and water pollution caused by intensive farming practices.

Finding better ways to use the land we have to grow the food we need is among the most pressing challenges of our time. That also makes it one of the biggest opportunities.

Regenerative farming – which uses practices that improve rather than destroy the ecosystem – can restore the health of soils and introduce the variety needed to support biodiversity. Perennial crops that don't need replanting each year keep soil healthier while using less fertilizer and energy. Vertical farms and insect farms can grow far more calories on far fewer hectares.

Matt Sexton, Futerra's Chief Transformation Officer, also often tells me that, 'precision fermentation is the future'. This is where bacteria are nudged into making any number of proteins, including those that look, taste and provide nutrients exactly like milk (without any cow's involvement). According to recent market research, the UK public is open to trying it (Thomas and Dillard, 2022).

Waste not, get more

Forty per cent of all the food that is grown is never eaten (WWF, 2021). Read that again. It is one of the most troubling environmental statistics I've heard, and the problem runs deep. Recent analysis has found that food loss and waste happens at every stage of food's journey from the farm to your fork. As much as 15 per cent is lost before it leaves the farm gate, and more goes to waste when it spoils as it travels to factories and packing centres (WWF, 2021). Yet more is wasted by supermarkets, and then by households who throw it out. In industrialized countries, this staggering food loss and waste costs $680 billion (UNEP, 2020). And saving just a quarter of it could prevent anyone from going hungry.

Solutions are on their way, in the form of packaging technologies that keep food fresher without the need for chilled lorries and the removal of 'best before' dates on groceries. What else is possible?

Eat it up

In Sweden, the MAX Burger sign is more common than the golden arches. Inside, you'll find carbon footprint data listed next to every burger and heavy promotion of plant-based meals. Sales of plant-based burgers skyrocketed 1,000 per cent between 2015 and 2018 from just 2 per cent up to 20 per cent of all meals sold (UNFCCC, 2019). Kaj Török, Chief Sustainability Officer at MAX Burgers, shared the secret with me: 'People love green burgers when they taste great. But please don't sell them as green alternatives – great burgers deserve great names!'

I can personally attest that their 'Grilloumi' burger is delicious.

Eat your green

Remember how 37 per cent of the world's greenhouse gas emissions are created by farming? Well over half of those emissions (57%) come from animal agriculture. Plant-based food production, on the other hand, accounts for less than a third (29%) (Xu et al, 2021). The science is clear: if we want to save the planet, we need to eat less meat and more plants.

This is well known, and many people have made the shift to veggie or vegan diets. Veganuary, the annual campaign to get people to go vegan for the month of January, breaks its own record each year (Hampson, 2022). Veg-friendly chefs like BOSH and Ottolenghi have become household names, and brands like Oomph!, THIS, Beyond Meat, Oatly and Impossible have skyrocketed to supermarket success.

Yet global meat consumption is still on the rise. It has doubled in the past couple of decades, and is forecast to rise by another 13 per cent by 2028. The Global North is responsible for the vast majority of meat-eating, with the average American, for example, eating 17 times more meat each year than the average Nigerian (Friends of the Earth, 2021).

There is so much further to go in adjusting diets to something more sustainable, and a growing number of ingredients that can help make it possible. Insect protein is set to become a staple, and emerging Solutionists highlight that genetically modified bacteria can be far more delicious than they sound.

Any success that plant-based alternatives have seen so far comes down to two very simple things: being desirable and feeling normal. How can you tempt more people to ditch meat and eat green? Succeed, and you'll be able to take a bite out of a market that's projected to be worth over $22 billion by 2025 (Wunsch, 2021).

You might ask yourself:

- How we use land isn't fair or efficient. Can you fix it?
- Who is going to crack transforming agriculture from carbon creator to carbon sink?
- We waste a third of all food. Are you the leader to monetize the solutions?
- Will you join the plant-based diet business leaders?

How's this for a recipe for a solid business plan: more safe and nutritious food reaching more people, with less waste and requiring fewer resources – a Solutionist dream.

5. The business of material solutions

Inventors, unite!

From carpets and crockery to toys and toothbrushes, our world is awash with stuff. Though some may be unnecessary – in consumerist cultures, at least – much of it is stuff we need to cook, bathe, socialize, live, work and sleep.

Making stuff is extractive of our natural resources, and all too often exploitative of the people who help source materials and manufacture products. The disposing of stuff – which we do to the tune of 2 billion tonnes every year – is equally damaging to the planet and the communities forced to live with everyone's waste (UNEP, 2009).

It doesn't have to be. There are cleaner, smarter, more efficient ways to make the things we use every day – we just need Solutionists to use them. Here are just some of the ways you could begin imagining a better materials future.

More, more, more

Trees, oil, crops, rocks, energy, water. The products we use depend on these and hundreds of other resources provided by the planet, many of which are difficult to replace. Which means using less of them should be a priority.

This could mean developing technology that can reduce the inputs needed, like denim brand DL1961 which has found a way to make jeans using just 10 gallons of water instead of 1,500 (DL1961, 2022). It could mean using recycled materials to limit the amount of virgin materials used, like Bureo's skateboards made from discarded fishing nets. Or it could mean putting waste to work, to prevent more resources being needed. Fashion brand Kalita, for example, use the fabric offcuts from their range of clothes to make knickers and face masks.

How can you make more with less?

Tomorrow stuff

Ever seen a building made of mushrooms? A leather couch made from grapes? How about diamonds made from pollution?

Many of the materials we see as the norm come at a huge cost. Concrete is responsible for 4–8 per cent of the world's CO_2 emissions (Olivier et al, 2016). Steel production is the most energy-consuming industrial activity in the world (The World Counts, 2020). Glass relies on mining raw materials like silica sand and dolomite that can release harmful pollution (Brock and Williams, 2020). Plastic is entering our oceans at a rate of 8 million tons a year (Jambeck et al, 2015), and it's estimated that humans are now ingesting 5 grams of it every week (Scarr, 2019).

Fortunately, there are new, ingenious materials making their way onto the scene every year. Unwanted potatoes are being turned into plastic. Discarded wool scraps are being collected and turned into durable chairs. Hemp is being used to make an alternative to concrete that's fire resistant and a good insulator.

Turning fur into furniture and plants into bricks might sound like magic, but it's just science. The possibilities are truly endless.

Live forever

Not you (that's a whole other topic...) – but the products you could make.

The idea of 'single use' was a new concept when it was introduced in the post-war period. People were used to economizing, reusing, 'make-do-and-mend'-ing, so getting used to disposability required a whole new attitude. It was an attitude that had to be taught – and taught it was, by the marketeers paid by big business to drive a shift that would power an economic boom. Their efforts were so effective that a poll in the 1940s rated 'cellophane' as the third most beautiful word in the English language (TIME, 1950).

While we are beginning to see a move away from single-use plastics, many products continue to be designed to have a limited lifespan. This is called 'planned obsolescence' and is particularly common for tech devices and appliances that are, essentially, built to break. New laws in the EU are forcing manufacturers to make products more easily fixable, and we should expect to see these regulations become more widespread. Just as society learnt a new way of using products in the 1940s, so we can learn – or relearn – a better way today.

The shift is underway to make products that can live forever. The world needs hairdryers that can be fixed once they're broken, and laptops with batteries that don't deteriorate. It needs smartphones, like the Fairphone, that can be repaired at home with a standard screwdriver; sofas, like the SofaForLife, that are made of individual parts that can be endlessly repaired and updated; and shoes, like

Birkenstocks, that the manufacturer will continue to repair for life. It needs easier ways to find a tailor, like SOJO or The Seam; and more repair services as an everyday staple of our communities and high streets.

Aside from the good it can do, the most exciting thing about these new approaches to materials is that they call for a whole new business model. So, put your inventor's hat on, and ask yourself:

- We need more from less. Can you design out materials that result in a better product?
- From mushroom leather to transparent wood, how will you take innovative/sustainable materials mainstream?
- Will you make repairing and extending the life of products the business model of the future?
- The circular economy is booming. Are you in the cycle?

The world of materials is your oyster. So, get inventing – you could create something that will live many lives.

6. The business of financial solutions

Where money goes, power follows. The direction and destination to which money travels determines everything about how our society works, and its relationship to the planet we live on. Today, inequalities mean that the richest 10 per cent of the population takes 52 per cent of global income; the poorest half take just 8 per cent (World Inequality Lab, 2022, p 10). This creates huge discrepancies in quality of life, and also means decision making lies in the hands of a few.

If it can reach different – and more – people's pockets, money can change lives and shift our collective priorities. Our economic and financial structures can feel behemothian, utterly entrenched, but there's more wiggle room than meets the eye. You don't have to be an accountant or a financial expert to spot where money, and power, is collecting in problematic places. To find ways to divert it, you do have to be a Solutionist.

Make money matter

More than $56 trillion is invested in pensions around the world (Thinking Ahead Institute, 2022). Around another $50 trillion is sitting in bank accounts (BIS 2020; CEIC 2022). This money isn't innocently waiting for its owner to withdraw it. Together, banks are pumping hundreds of billions of dollars a year into fossil fuels. Stop this cash flow, and these destructive industries will soon run out of steam.

Alternative models of investing – including ESG investing, patient capital and impact investing – are well established. Banks like Triodos, Co-op and Fiare Banca Etica, for example, offer ways for people to make sure their money is invested in ways that don't fuel harm. Charity Bank uses its savers' money solely to lend to charities and social enterprises. And investor networks like GenderSmart are using finance to support gender equality.

There's still a long way to go before the financial pipeline to the world's most damaging forces runs dry. We need more people to be aware of what their money is doing, and to feel confident that they can do something about it.

Move it around

There might be a lot of money sitting in bank accounts, but not everyone has one. In fact, 24 per cent of people are unbanked, and women are less likely to have a bank account than men (Demirguc-Kunt et al, 2021). No bank means no access to credit or to a mortgage; it means missing out on cheaper utility bills, mobile phone deals and personal loans. A low or no credit score can also make it even more difficult to cover healthcare costs.

There are barriers to banking that, once tackled, could empower people in their millions. In the United States alone, nearly 4 million people live in 'banking deserts', areas without a nearby bank branch. How can in-person banking reach rural areas and lower-income communities, and how can digital banking better bridge the gap?

Patient finance is a crucial part of this picture. Being able to pay for expensive treatments monthly rather than up front can be the difference between life and death. A US survey found that nearly two-thirds of people want access to a payment plan but just 44 per cent of people have been offered one (PYMNTS, 2021). People are missing out on care, and healthcare providers are losing revenue. Solutions here could save lives.

Balance the planet's books

Neither the causes nor the consequences of climate change are evenly spread around the globe. It's well known that the countries most responsible for historical emissions – most notably the United States, followed by the EU, China and Russia – are not the ones suffering its worst effects. These are felt most dramatically and consistently in poorer countries, in the forms of floods, droughts, extreme heat and storms. Forests are destroyed, coastlines lost, homes washed away.

Campaigners have long called for rich, polluting countries to pay for this loss and damage, and the conversation was brought into the mainstream at 2022's COP27 climate conference. There is urgency and energy behind the need to address loss and damage, and the field is open for solutions. The world needs initiatives that harness local expertise to support developing economies; use tech and finance in new ways to help more people, more quickly; and that collect important data that can help measure what matters beyond money, like losses to cultural heritage and damage to health.

These are just some of the starting points you might consider when tackling the huge forces that lie beneath our global financial systems:

- Can you bring banking, insurance and finance to the 1 billion people without it?
- Will patient finance unlock long-term investment in the solutions?
- Who sees the opportunity for climate loss-and-damage restitutions to spark economic energy across the world?

Get imaginative about financial solutions, and you can get right to the heart of some of the world's biggest, most deeply rooted problems. New ideas will come in many forms – they could be digital tools, smart collaborations, imaginative measurement solutions, or whole new models that rethink value and prioritize people and planet. Finance is a huge lever for change. Could you help pull it?

7. The business of nature-based solutions

It makes sense that some of the most effective ways to save the planet involve working with the planet. Futuristic technologies have their place, but nature's existing systems are already built to keep life going. Harness life's own power, and we can slow down damage to our environment and the communities that depend on it (hint: that's all of us).

Nature's systems are vast and beautifully complex. Here are just some of the ways that climate and biodiversity solutions can team up with them.

Lock it up

Forests and fens, marshes and mangroves, peatlands and permafrost. These and other life-rich types of land are the unsung powerhouses of our fight against climate change. They trap carbon in their rich soil, keeping it out of the atmosphere. And let's not forget the ocean, whose phytoplankton absorb around the same amount of carbon as all the plants and trees on land combined.

Pollution and pressures on the world's available land mean that these ecosystems are under threat. With the right protections and creative solutions, we can preserve – and expand – these crucial carbon sinks. Rewetting wetlands can fill dried-out land with life again and keep carbon in the ground by the hundreds of gigatonnes. Restorative agriculture can transform over-farmed fields into healthy, carbon-trapping land. And regrowing forests can turn wastelands into environmental wonderlands.

Governments and businesses are looking for more ways to sequester carbon – how can you help them do it? Ecotourism and sustainable farming are just some of the ways that intact ecosystems can provide financial value – what other models can you create?

Species solutions

The health of our planet is reliant on its ecosystems' complexity. Namely, the number of species of plants, animals and insects that keep life going, all constantly balancing and supporting each other in a millennia-old dance of survival and symbiosis. Human activity – like pollution, overfishing and habitat destruction – means that the current extinction rate is estimated to be somewhere between 1,000 to 10,000 times higher than it would be if humans didn't exist (De Vos et al, 2014). We are losing life at an unprecedented rate.

The best protectors of the world's biodiversity are indigenous communities, who steward the land they live on. They are currently doing the vital work of safeguarding 80 per cent of the world's remaining biodiversity (Sobrevila, 2008). It is crucial that environmental solutions support them, and don't – as many well-intentioned initiatives do – drive them from their land.

According to the UN Environment Program, every dollar invested in restoration creates up to $30 in economic benefits (UNEP, 2021, p 3). This is an extraordinary opportunity. What part will you play in this new, nature-positive economy?

- Nature is our best ally in solving climate change. What's your plan for natural carbon sinks?
- Business wisdom teaches us the rarer something is, the higher its value. How can you prove the value of endangered biodiversity?

- Indigenous and traditional communities protect the planet's remaining biodiversity. How can you value that service?
- The market for restoring and repairing environmental damage is growing. Are you part of it?

Businesses and governments are slowly catching on to the financial value held in healthy natural systems, so now is the time to offer ways for them to harness it. And future solutions will formulate new models, beyond finance, that measure wellbeing, health, even beauty as part of the balance sheet. These kinds of reframings and reimaginings are as challenging as they are exciting – which means we need all the Solutionists we can get.

8. The business of digital solutions

It goes without saying that technology has, after a brief period of lightning-fast cultural adaptation, completely integrated into our lives. A mere 40 years ago, emails, smartphones, tweets and non-fungible tokens (NFTs) were the stuff of science fiction. I know, because I'm almost exactly the same age as the internet.

Here are just some of the ways you can begin thinking about how to harness the power of pixels.

Digital eyes and ears

Technology can multiply our ability to look and listen for important data that helps us understand social and environmental problems – and the information we need to solve them. Drones are already being used to collect crucial data about the world's rainforests (Imperial College London, 2020), and tiny sensors can detect details of a factory environment so that it can make real-time adjustments to minimize energy usage (Business Norway, 2018).

Just as early warning systems for earthquakes can quickly alert a population about an upcoming tremor, so too could technology offer ways to predict other, ever-more-common, natural disasters so that people can adapt or escape (NASA, 2016).

Even small tweaks can have huge impacts. Google Maps now plots both the fastest, and also most fuel-efficient, route when you plan a journey by car. Sounds like a trivial change? In one year, those changes helped avoid an estimate of more than half a million metric tons of carbon emissions – that's equivalent to taking approximately 100,000 fuel-based cars off the road (Google, 2022). Often, these digital solutions use this power of tiny adjustments at a huge scale in ways many of us might not spot in our daily lives.

The speed we need

The brilliant folks at the Exponential Roadmap Initiative have identified that right now, digital technologies could help reduce global carbon emissions by as much as 15 per cent (2019). They also outline where technology itself is advancing exponentially: 5G, for example, is between 10 and 100 times faster than 4G, and is more reliable while also consuming less energy (Ericsson, 2017). New possibilities will cascade from each breakthrough: remote working will become more effective, virtual replications of physical objects known as 'digital twins' will become more widely used, and leisure will move further online as the metaverse expands.

As these step-changes happen, they will open the possibility of similarly rapid progress for the solutions they enable.

Access for all

The digital world removes some of the barriers of the physical world. When it comes to education, for example, scalability makes offerings vastly more affordable, and the emissions (and jetlag) associated with travelling to in-person classes and conferences disappear. We are already seeing Massive Open Online Courses (MOOCs) offer free online education for career development and lifelong learning. Globally, the number of online learners more than doubled between 2019 and 2021 (Coursera, 2021).

Technology also opens up trade, connecting buyers with sellers of all sizes. Online platforms can, for example, link farmers directly to buyers, bypassing middlemen that increase prices and underpay growers (Mezzanine, 2020).

Status symbols, but not as we know them

Human beings are status-driven creatures. Where once we showed off our wealth and social prowess through flashy cars, fancy watches and expensive diamonds, we are now beginning to turn towards their digital equivalents. The world's first digital dress sold for $9,500 (The Fabricant, 2020). This is just the beginning of a new world of digital showing off, where polluting products are forgotten in favour of pixels.

Of course, the digital world doesn't currently exist without its own climate impact. Powering data centres and devices relies on vast amounts of electricity, and devices themselves are carbon-costly to manufacture. It is estimated that digital technologies contribute between 1.4 and 5.9 per cent of global greenhouse gas emissions (The Royal Society, 2020). Hopefully, these environmental downsides could soon be a thing of the past. We are experiencing the eco-equivalent of teething problems – the early blip of difficulties that get ironed out. Moving to renewables will decarbonize electricity production, and in an exciting recent breakthrough, the Ethereum blockchain – which previously had a carbon footprint comparable to the whole of Switzerland's – cut its energy usage by more than 99 per cent with just a tweak of its algorithm (Ethereum, 2022).

Web3 is about to multiply the opportunities for digital solutions to sustainability challenges. We will see decentralized blockchain technology completely overturn the way we trade and where we ascribe value. Dealing in bits and bytes instead of nature's precious 'offline' resources opens up a world of possibilities.

What will you do with them?

- Can you substitute 'real world' products with dematerialized ones online? Making money without making stuff?
- Where can data and artificial intelligence (AI) speed our understanding of how the world is changing?

- Can you digitize adaptation, helping communities across the world cope with change?
- In Web3 we will tokenize intangibles. Can you give nature worth in that world?
- Billions need access to information. Are you going to democratize data?

Back in 2007, the top 10 biggest companies in the world included just one tech firm. One short decade later, tech companies made up half the list (Financial Times, 2007, 2017). The opportunities are dizzying.

9. The business of cultural solutions

Climate change is equally a crisis of culture as it is of chemistry, which means that culture can also come to the rescue of the climate. The 2022 IPCC report I've referenced before, calculates that 'behaviour and sociocultural' changes could rapidly save 5 per cent of all demand-side carbon emissions. In climate terms, that's a huge win – if we can make it happen (IPCC, 2022).

Thankfully, we have a global industry in the business of culture. The 'creative economy' of arts, culture and entertainment contributes just over 6 per cent of global GDP (Lorente, 2016), and according to the UN, it generates annual revenues of over $2 trillion, including nearly 50 million jobs worldwide (UNESCO, 2017). TV is the largest part of that creative economy in terms of revenue, while visual arts and music are the largest industries in terms of employment (over half their employees are women) (EY, 2015).

That a lot of talent, creativity, imagination and influence that can be put in service of solutions.

Scope X

On 31 March 1929, a young woman stepped out into a bustling New York street at the height of the Easter Day Parade. She lit up a Lucky Strike cigarette, provoking gasps of outrage. Ten other women followed her down the street, brandishing their new 'torches of freedom'. An early example of spontaneous feminism perhaps? In fact, it was an early example of the power of advertising. The women had been hired by Edward Bernays, the father of advertising (and nephew to psychologist Sigmund Freud). Their gesture of liberation was engineered in front of a waiting audience of journalists, and the story spread across America. Bernays' masterstroke was a resounding success: sales of cigarettes among women soared (Lee, 2008).

I call this influence 'Scope X', and the two-trillion-dollar advertising industry wields a lot of it (Townsend, 2021).

We need to turn the tide of Scope X impacts. The fossil-fuel industry has ploughed a whopping US$1.4 billion into PR and advertising over the past decade, six times more than they spent on renewable energy interests (Climate Investigations Center, 2019). That ratio makes one thing clear: the advertising industry is putting the weight of its creativity behind the causes of the climate emergency. Instead, we need all those creative directors, graphic designers, ideators and 'architects of desire' to divest their talent from destruction.

If you can sell shampoo, you can sell solar panels, and if you can make cars sexy, what about bikes? Every solution in this chapter needs advertising help. Anyway, selling the solutions is the greatest creative challenge of our age. Why wouldn't you want to be in on that?

All change

The IPCC has our thanks for synthesizing nearly 7,000 academic papers on actions that can truly make a difference – they have identified over 61 actions that can save significant and measurable amounts from consumers' carbon footprint – up to nine tonnes per person.

Changing how we travel is the biggest behavioural win, as individual choices could save 15 per cent of all travel carbon (for the avoidance of doubt, that is a huge amount), followed by eating less meat and buying sustainable stuff.

Leaders, brands and influencers have the power to support consumers in making these lifestyle changes to solve the climate crisis. With a bit of creativity, mixed with a lot of behavioural science, creatives can help culture change rather than climate change:

- Are you the media mogul who can crack selling the sustainability story?
- Will you wield the power of positive advertising to change what's desirable?
- Consumers want help to change behaviours. Can you build the business model to help them?

Futerra ran a survey which revealed an overwhelming demand from consumers for brands to step up on sustainable lifestyles. Fail to do that and we're in danger of disappointing 88 per cent of them. The survey also tells us that 43 per cent of consumers believe that brands are mostly making it harder for them to be more sustainable. This desire for a sustainable lifestyle continues to rise exponentially. In June 2020, Google Trends revealed a 4,550 per cent increase in searches on 'how to live a sustainable lifestyle' (BITC, 2020).

Are you ready?

These ideas haven't even scratched the surface of what's out there! I hope at least I've got your Solutionist juices flowing.

EXERCISE   Solutions starters

If you already work in a company or industry, or have a plan for one, the very best way to discover a breakthrough solution is to invent your competitor.

I've run this exercise with leadership teams from small start-ups to major multinationals, and every single time the solutions soared:

1   Imagine you're a start-up founder pitching for investment from a super-wealthy solutions-obsessed VC.

2   Look at how the market is changing, what the Solutions Economy might bring, where the opportunities are.

3   Then, design a well-funded disruptor brand that will use sustainable solutions to outcompete your current company.

We often run this session over several days offsite, but even an evening doodling on a pad can generate valuable ideas using this approach.

Because the best competitor is, always, yourself.

CHAPTER SEVEN

The quarter rule

I'm old enough to remember spraying chlorofluorocarbons (CFCs) on my hair. In my defence, hairspray was a big deal in the 1980s. For a long time, CFCs were thought to be a 'perfect chemical'. As a non-flammable and non-toxic substance, they were used in refrigerators, fire extinguishers, air conditioners and, yes, in aerosols like hairspray.

Then, in the 1970s, scientists discovered that when CFCs reach the atmosphere, ultraviolet radiation breaks them down, releasing chlorine. That chlorine combined with the oxygen in our air is devastatingly destructive to the ozone layer. Our fragile skins are protected from the sun's radiation by a thin layer of ozone – which we'd already torn a hole in. A few countries, Canada, Sweden and the United States, unilaterally banned the use of

CFCs in aerosols. That wasn't enough to pull us back into a safe zone.

Then, one of the main producers of CFCs, the US company DuPont, invented safer substitutes for CFCs, and the company went from lobbying against banning CFCs to actually supporting their phasing out. The CFC story also made its way into public consciousness – led especially by the people most at risk from skin cancer caused by the thinning hole. Boycotts of hairspray and other CFC-containing products were a fixture of 1980s life, and the science of the ozone hole started to be raised in everything from nightly news to children's programming and even jokes in sitcoms.

Taken together, these factors reached a 'tipping point' of public anxiety and political pressure, leading countries to negotiate 'The Montreal Protocol on Substances that Deplete the Ozone Layer'. That agreement remains one of the fastest-negotiated and most effective global agreements in history.

Our essential ozone layer has been healing ever since and is on track to be fully restored somewhere between 2040 and 2070 (UN, 2019).

How we closed the ozone hole is a great story for Solutionists. It encompasses breakthrough innovation, entrepreneurial action, political change and social campaigns, all to solve a seemingly intractable and terrifying environmental crisis – and it worked.

It's also an example of how pressure builds and builds, until suddenly something has to give and change speeds to exponential levels.

Our societies go through these S-curves of support for issues or in the spread of behaviours more often than you might think. In both the UK and the United States, support for same-sex marriage bumped along in surveys at very minimal levels for generations, then backing leapt to over 30 per cent in under a decade (Tribou and Collins, 2015). Soon after, equal marriage became law. That wasn't an accident or slow build of support – it was a planned and very effective campaign to prove tipping-point levels of voter interest in the topic. As the US Supreme Court took up arguments in key marriage rights cases in 2013, a red 'equal' sign released by the Human Rights Campaign replaced more than 15 million profile pictures on social media platforms. The tipping point of support was visible to policymakers and public alike.

Researchers in the United States have tracked other swift changes in opinion that spark action, from prohibition and women's suffrage through to legalization of marijuana. All of them non-linear curves – where a certain level of support built from nothing and then swiftly cascaded into wide social acceptance.

Paul Polman, former CEO of Unilever, explained his experience of the phenomena as:

> You know, the famous African proverb, 'If you want to go fast, you go alone. If you want to go far, you go together.' Where I spent most of my time, in this respect, is bringing CEOs together at critical mass across the value chain, so they actually become more courageous together. And not surprisingly, you know, you start with $37 trillion of money in companies' market cap making net-zero commitments

and science-based targets, then you have $57 trillion of the finance community really net zero-ing their portfolios. Now you have 65 per cent of the countries, but since they're big countries, 95 per cent of the carbon emissions covered by net-zero agreements. So, things are starting to move, so sustainability becomes an easier sell now than what it was before.

For Solutionists, understanding and learning how to ignite these tipping points is crucial. In business we benefit from them, and for sustainability, the world needs positive tipping points, and it needs them now. We can't just sit around and hope they happen, we've got to get involved.

What's the point?

There has been much debate over the past decades about how many people have to move their opinion or behaviour before a tipping point happens – and everyone else comes on board.

The IPCC scientists put the societal level of change needed to 'ignite' a tipping point anywhere between 10 and 30 per cent (IPCC, 2022). That's quite a large margin for anyone trying to transform a business, industry or community. Activists have claimed it takes only 3.5 per cent of a population to get involved in a campaign to create serious political change (Chenoweth, 2013). According to famed author of the *Tipping Point* book, Malcolm Gladwell, it's somewhere around 10 per cent of a population, the threshold at which a committed minority adopting new behaviours can change the social norm and pull the silent majority along with it (Gladwell, 2000). Others have pointed out that no system can claim to have 'tipped' until 51 per cent, a mathematical majority, of people are doing/agreeing/behaving in the same way (Roberts, 2007).

All these numbers are subject to context, of course. If 3.5 per cent of a population (which in the UK is 2.4 million people) sat outside the Houses of Parliament demanding change, it would have a bigger impact than if 10 per cent of us posted about the same issue online.

The lack of clarity over the percentage has held many changemakers back from using tipping-point strategies to plan their work.

Thankfully, the first quantifiable research into tipping points was recently undertaken by academics at the University of Pennsylvania. The researchers recruited volunteers and separated them into different online groups. Then, they asked the different groups to 'pick a name' for someone in an un-named photo. Everyone jumped in with ideas, generating various names. Then the volunteers were incentivized to come to consensus on a single name – which each group did. This led to what scientists call a stable 'social norm'. Everyone had agreed to something and were using that name in their online conversations.

The scientists then 'activated' different percentages of people in each group – to try to change the name. The 'activists' suggested that the name be changed, all suggesting the same new name. But 3.5 per cent of people calling for a new name made no difference, they were ignored, nor did 10 per cent, or 20 per cent, all the way up to... 25 per cent. Once a quarter of people called for the new name – everyone agreed, even though the group was incentivized to keep the old name. This 25 per cent threshold happened in group after group.

One of the most interesting parts of the study is how close you can come to changing everything. At 22 or 23 per cent of people agreeing, buying or doing something, you might still be struggling and perhaps even give up – without knowing that just a few more voices joining would hit the magic number (Centola et al, 2018)! Understanding this magic 25 per cent tipping point, and what can get us there, should matter to Solutionists. In the coming years, unexpected opportunities will open, new markets and new products will be needed, social change will speed up. And to solve climate change we'll need multiple tipping points in every society. Incremental change simply isn't moving us fast enough; it's time for some big tips.

Why 25 per cent?

The quarter number is much higher than some of the previous estimates of what it takes to really tip change. There are lots of theories about why we need so many other people to do something before everyone does it.

The main one is that the 'social cost' to individuals of doing something 'new' drops at that 25 per cent point. Before then, you might look weird, or feel silly doing/buying/believing something if too few others do the same. At 25 per cent you have safety in numbers and eventually, after 50 per cent is passed, the social cost works the other way, because now you're the majority. A society reaches this 'tipping threshold' when the proportion of people deviating from the norm becomes large enough that even individuals who are risk averse, conformist, or have pessimistic expectations about the prospects of change have an incentive to follow suit.

Not all change requires entire populations to tip. You might be seeking a tipping point within your business, to reach 25 per cent of your colleagues. Or you might have a target group of consumers, a specific community or even a set of experts you're trying to 'tip'.

Getting to a quarter of people, even in a small community, might feel daunting. Thankfully, in addition to measuring the percentage it takes to tip, social scientists have carefully analysed social change, technology spread and consumer behaviour.

There are two leverage points that stand head-and-shoulders over every other in terms of activating change. If you can master them, then you'll master the art of creating tips:

- Benefits. The primary factor in most tipping points is when enough people understand and accept the personal benefits from change. Not collective benefits. Not environmental benefits. But the very literal, 'what's in it for me?'.
- Perseverance. As Solutionists, we already know tenacity is our gift. And all the research shows that tipping points depended on a group of leaders who persist in moving against the established equilibrium, even in the face of pushback.

Sell the benefits of change, and don't give up – that sounds like something Solutionists can get on board with. Yet, in my experience, the first lever is too often underestimated or forgotten in the story of change.

Who tipped the electric car?

Will Ferrell hates Norway, at least according to an advert first aired during one of the coveted Superbowl advertising slots in 2021. The famous comic's ire at Norway is because electric cars sell more there than in the United States. Riffing off America's legendary competitive spirit, Ferrell punches a globe and vows that America will beat Norway in EV sales, which might be possible if the United States follows the Norwegian tipping-point plan.

Almost 65 per cent of new passenger cars sold in Norway in 2021 were electric and a further 22 per cent were plug-in hybrids. That means only 14 per cent of new cars were sold without a plug. It took the Norwegians only 10 years to move from near-zero EV sales to this 65 per cent, and in 2022 over 80 per cent of cars sold in Norway will be EVs. It's been an astonishing tip for a country without a history of vehicle innovation (at time of writing, Norway has no car-manufacturing factories on its soil) (Norsk Elbilforening, 2022).

It takes time to electrify all the cars on the road. Most cars are purchased second-hand, and people in the second-hand market are dependent on the choices made by new-car buyers. To spur the switch, the Norwegian government taxes sales of new polluting cars heavily but does not tax

EVs at all, making EVs, which are often more expensive because of their production costs, a no-brainer for most Norwegians. The Norwegian parliament also decided that all sales of new cars and vans must be zero emission by 2025, making it a risky choice to buy a car with an exhaust considering you might not be able to sell it on.

This isn't exclusively a Norwegian phenomenon. While Norway took 2.5 years to move from 2 to 10 per cent EV market share, the UK took 1.5 years and Germany only one. President Biden's infrastructure bill includes $7.5 billion for a nationwide charging network in the United States (Bu, 2022). And according to Ernst and Young, 52 per cent of global car buyers want an electric vehicle (Ernst & Young, 2022).

Norway didn't start this ball rolling. In fact, all governments are playing catch-up with a change that was already underway.

In 1997 Toyota launched the Prius, the first modern mass-manufactured hybrid. Marketed as a green choice, the Prius was the poster child of eco-aware celebrities for years. The Prius is a great little car, compact and friendly. But no one would call it sexy and the boasting rights of having one were mainly to prove your environmental credentials.

Then Tesla launched the Roadster. Designed with gliders from iconic supercar brand Lotus, with a top speed of 125 miles per hour, the first-ever Roadster advert, aired in 2007 (now with over a million views online), showed sleek black and red Roadsters speeding through gritty, graffitied, urban jungles to a pounding electronic backing track. This car was the cool, leather-jacketed, smoking behind the bike-sheds kid compared to the goody-two-shoes prim Prius.

If 'selling the benefits' is the best way to trigger the quarter of any community to desire change, Tesla went all-in on that desire, benefit and a waiting list for their sports cars. Branding the electric car's acceleration as 'insane mode' and building a Star-Trek-esque dashboard firmly placed Tesla's car in the 'for motor heads' rather than 'for tree huggers' camp.

Too often, changemakers jump immediately to the 'get governments to regulate this to happen', before getting the 'make sure people want this to happen' stage right.

When you're planning your tipping-point strategy, product, business or global domination, remember that 'sell the personal benefit' comes before anything else.

Plant-based power

Several years ago, while chairing a large conference in the United States, I was asked to taste an Impossible Burger live on stage. I almost spat it out.

Because I'm a vegetarian and with the added 'heme' flavour that Impossible invented, their burger tastes just too much like meat for my tastes. I honestly thought someone had substituted beef into that burger!

Of course, those were the early days of Impossible and before the 'plant-based' tip started, one which we are arguably still in. Our complex global food system, with millions of products and processes, is far more complex than the car industry. But the tip within this sprawling and incomprehensibly large system is hard to ignore. More than 25 per cent of Europeans now consider themselves 'flexitarian', vegetarian or vegan (Smart Protein Project, 2021), and according to the Good Food Institute, the sales of plant-based foods grew three times faster than overall food sales in 2021 (Good Food Institute, 2022). Beyond Meat and Impossible Foods are the top two contenders for global market value among alternative protein companies, the first estimated to be worth 9 billion dollars in 2021, and the latter valued at 7 billion dollars in February 2022 (Roof and Tan, 2021).

Today, across Europe, and increasingly in the United States and beyond, plant-based meals and options are in every supermarket and on most restaurant menus.

From a sustainability point of view this is excellent news. According to the United Nations, almost a quarter of global greenhouse gas emissions comes from agriculture, with livestock being one of the main contributors. Livestock's emissions include methane (yep, burps and farts), which is up to 34 times more damaging to the climate than carbon dioxide (IPCC, 2015). In the past half-century, global meat production has increased by more than 400 per cent. It's no wonder that the IPCC puts 'eating less meat' as one of the top actions that individuals can take to reduce emissions (IPCC, 2022).

Plant-based foods are an excellent example of a tipping point that's had barely any policymaker/government support and which food companies had to scramble to keep up with rather than lead. Politicians might be prepared to put extra taxes on polluting cars, and give EVs incentives, but few are prepared to do the same for meat. The long arc of tipping towards plant-based foods has been primarily led by stories.

Of course, veganism has been around for centuries in different guises. Across the world there are religious and cultural communities, large ones, that eschew meat. In contrast, in the EU and United States, veganism was at best a 'specialist' interest with very few options sold only in health food shops, at worst a butt of jokes.

Then, on Google Trends you can see searches for 'plant based' start to creep up from around 2011. One reason for this growing interest was the popular documentary, 'Forks Over Knives', which dug into the health benefits of a wholegrain, natural and no-meat diet. In societies where 'non-communicable diseases' are the top cause of death, for example heart disease and diabetes, the promise of health through food proved appealing.

There's another jump in searches when 'Cowspiracy' came out in 2014. This shocking documentary was almost a 'body horror' film in the uncompromising view of how mega-farms actually operate and what that means you're actually eating.

The exponential line on the Google searches graph doesn't start until 2018, coinciding with the Netflix documentary, 'The Game Changers'. With executive producers including Jackie Chan, Arnold Schwarzenegger, Novak Djokovic and Lewis Hamilton, this film portrays plant-based eating to be the equivalent of a wonder drug. Want firmer abs, smarter thinking, better sleep, a beautiful body and a serene mind? Go plant-based. The film was wildly popular with audiences, especially health and fitness-focused ones, who until that point had assumed meat protein was essential for health.

With cage-fighters and body builders obsessed with plant-based eating, the 'weedy' image of veganism was finally put to bed. And, of course, that all-important ingredient – a personal benefit – was added in. Eating less meat was now better for the animals, the planet – and me.

In 2022, 620,000 people globally signed up for Veganuary, compared with just 250,000 in 2019 (Veganuary). And in the UK, the high-street low-cost takeaway icon, Greggs, introduced a vegan sausage roll with such fanfare it trended on Twitter for days.

You can see how this tip keeps rolling. More people want planet based, so more supermarkets offer it in the aisles, leading to more people trying plant-based, so restaurants have to offer plant-based options, leading to… Hit the tip, and your issue, product, business or campaign becomes self-sustaining.

One plant-based product that has firmly tipped is plant-based milk. Around the world, the estimated per capita consumption of plant-based milk has grown from half a kilogram in 2013 to nearly a full kilogram in 2020. Meanwhile, the overall worldwide consumption of milk substitutes almost doubled from 3.7 billion kilograms in 2013 to 6.3 billion kilograms in 2020 (Statista, 2021).

Back in 1994, brothers Rickard and Björn Öste formulated their first version of an oat-based milk, Oatly, and tried to peddle their wares to a big dairy company. The head of R&D at the big company spat it out, calling it 'unsellable'.

In 2012, two team members joined the company – Toni Petersson as CEO and John Schoolcraft as Creative Director – who would put Oatly's well-established health and environmental benefits in the spotlight. They set out Oatly's strategy: to create good in the world while being, in their words, 'fucking fearless'. They weren't shy about undermining the dairy industry, and plastered slogans including 'like milk, but made for humans' across billboards. Dairy firms didn't like it and took Oatly to court. The result was more press, more sales and an estimated $41 million in profit by 2015.

In 2016, Oatly launched in the United States. By 2018, it was available in 20 countries – and so popular that there wasn't enough of it to go around. They swiftly built a 19,000-square-foot factory in New Jersey, just to keep up.

The United States led to Asia, and milk led to other dairy alternatives: custard, cream, creme fraiche. Oatly became one of the first brands to state its CO_2 footprint on the pack and has launched petitions to make other brands do the same. Their irreverence gave them permission to make otherwise worthy environmental claims. They did something that hadn't been done before: they made the 'green' choice the fun choice.

Toni, the CEO, is definitely a fun person to interview. When I asked him what a film of his life would be like, he answered that the frantic pace of the spy-thriller television show '24' came to mind: 'It's like a race against the clock, the task you have as a business leader. But also a race against the clock in terms of climate change, right? Every morning I wake up with a bunch of complex problems that need quick decisions. Some backfire, some don't. 24 is the life I live right now – and I've done that throughout my whole life. Because the world of consumer-facing business is wildly, and wonderfully, unpredictable.'

Thankfully, he assured me it didn't involve any kidnappings or hanging out of helicopters. Toni calls the sceptics of sustainable business, 'bland, binary and blindly naïve', and has a clear vision of how to take his tipping point all the way:

> I'm impatient, but every day I think, 'Okay, how do we solve this?' We all live within a system, whether this be economic, political, cultural or religious – our societies are a whole. And we're going to change things by including and communicating with everyone, without condemning or judging too quickly. Everybody speaks about how fucked up things are, but, knowing that we exist within a system, what in that system should we focus on trying to fix? And how do we include everyone in the benefits of that?

For Toni, success means bringing people together to make the necessary changes so everybody gets a better life. As he says, 'You can't be happy unless people around you are happy, you know?'

Toni is an excellent business leader. When Oatly floated on the public stock market in 2020, it was valued at $10 billion. And he knows that to change everything, it's going to take everyone benefitting.

The other type of tip

This whole chapter is about generating positive tipping points that work for us. By selling benefits, persevering, and getting 25 per cent of a community, consumer group or society to join us, we can cascade our solutions into the mainstream. It's an exciting and important idea.

Unfortunately, it would be remiss of me to write about tipping points without mentioning the ones we don't want as well as the ones we do.

Humanity has already tipped our climate to 1.1 degrees of warming. And the world's scientists agree that 1.5 degrees is the only 'sort-of-safe' level that we should absolutely throw everything at staying within. That's because even at 1.1 degrees a few things – like ice caps and ocean currents – get a bit wobbly (IPCC, 2021). At 2 degrees of change, according to my friends at the Potsdam Institute for Climate Impact Research, we create a domino effect that no one wants (Wunderling et al, 2021). The Amazon would tip from lush forest to burnt savannah, the billions of tonnes of water trapped in the Greenland icesheet would melt and that water would flood our coastal cities; we would lose our coral reefs, which could wreck the fish stocks that so much of humanity depends upon.

There are many, excellent and terrifying, books about these too-close-for-comfort tipping-point risks. Not least about how triggering one might change our biosphere so much that it triggers the others.

The University of Exeter in the UK hosted an extraordinary conference about tipping points in 2022. Gathering both climate scientists and social scientists, many of the world's leading brains on tipping points set out both the terrible tipping points the planet might face and the radical social tipping points that might prevent that happening. Like so many climate events, sitting in on the sessions I felt overwhelmed by the sheer scale of the climate tipping points and the incomprehensible damage and suffering they would cause. After nearly three decades of listening to this stuff, it still feels like a sucker punch to confront it head on. The scale and speed of change urgently needed makes you take a big gulp and dredge up every last solution you can think of.

However, one factor emerged in our favour that comforted and inspired me. Both the climate and the social scientists agreed at the conference that nature and society operate on very different timescales, and that might just change everything.

People change faster than the planet. Natural cycles can tip, disastrously, but it takes time – that Greenland ice sheet isn't going to disappear tomorrow.

We could change tomorrow, though. What social science teaches us is that our behaviours and even beliefs are much more flexible that we might admit. Massive social tipping points have happened within our own lifetimes and will again. Rolling out solutions can be non-linear and tomorrow can look very different from today. We're in a race to what will tip first – us or nature. It's a race we need to win.

EXERCISE   Solutions starters

In addition to the massive levers of selling the benefits and persevering, researchers offer us other tools and insights to get our desired tipping points:

1   Increasing returns. There is a speeding effect in tipping points. As more and more people adopt a behaviour or technology, it becomes more attractive (in quality or price). This is very obvious with EVs as more people buy them, more charging points are built, making it easier for

---

others to buy them, and so on. As you roll out your new solution, keep watching for those increasing returns and make sure to highlight them to potential consumers/ audiences.

2   Learning by doing. Often, the more something is done/ made, the better it can be done/made. Many solutions are in early stage, R&D or still being tested. Many of us aren't professional chefs; perhaps we only know how to cook 5–6 meals well, and we like to stick to them. When going plant based we need to relearn those meals or add new recipes to our weekly plans. By offering recipe advice, more people can try a plant-based diet. Often offering a 'trial' of a behaviour, product or idea can speed uptake.

3   Technological reinforcement. The more something is used, the more technologies emerge that make it more useful. From mobile phone apps to EV charging points, most technologies need supporting ones. Seek to enable the supporting technologies for your solution to speed reaching the tipping point.

4   Informational cascades. Massive media and communications pushes can prove to people that the behaviour/product/belief you're pushing is socially accepted and 'normal'. Once you're getting close to 25%, you need to look mainstream rather than alternative.

CHAPTER EIGHT

Storytelling the solutions

You sit, face illuminated only by your laptop screen, doing your research. It's time to buy a new family car, and you're going to make an informed decision. This is probably the single biggest expense for your family this year. On top of that, last night your daughter looked up at you as you tucked her in; 'We're getting a car that's good for the planet, aren't we?' she asked, her big anxious eyes adding another thing to your research list. You spend long hours comparing miles-per-hour stats, carbon footprints and safety-test results. By morning you're sure, you've got the facts, you've picked the perfect EV.

Then, at work, a rather annoying colleague from a different department starts chatting while you both wait for the coffee machine. In passing you mention your well-researched and rational choice. The annoying colleague raises an eyebrow. 'Oh no, don't do that. My brother-in-law's cousin had hell with that car. Stuck with loads of maintenance costs. Wouldn't risk it, if I were you.'

Even though you've heard only one, apocryphal, story versus all the objective facts you've diligently researched – according to psychologists, in that situation you won't buy the car you previously chose (Freling et al, 2020).

Why would people be that irrational, after finding the facts? Because human beings have been shown, over and over again (and despite believing we're rational), that we believe stories over statistics, especially when dealing with severe threats like climate change or anything that might affect us personally (Freling et al, 2020).

In fact (excuse the irony), according to research by Stanford University, 'Stories are remembered up to 22 times more than facts alone' (Bruner, 1986). That's why every politician leads with anecdotes rather than analysis. Why charities tell the story of one victim of disaster rather than the cold statistics of loss. Why brands weave stories through their advertising messages.

Solutionists must become storytellers. Because, however great your solution is, without a story, you'll never sell it to anyone.

Change the story, save the world

Climate change is now communicating itself – the floods carrying cars past roof tops, fires burning to the edge of cityscapes, the white swirl of a hurricane seen from space, and emaciated polar bears clinging to a chip of melting ice.

Those impacts need no storyteller other than our eyes. Running through this harsh reality is a 'metanarrative' in how we frame these impacts. Currently, that metanarrative is reinforcing a terrible message. It's a morality play, playing out like Frankenstein – man makes monster, then monster destroys man.

For too many people, climate change has become like a movie when you know the characters are heading towards a tragic ending, but none of them can do anything about it! That climate mortality play is in danger of becoming a self-fulfilling prophesy in real life.

The climate-Frankenstein story is creeping into people's psyche, sucking the will to act from them. Futerra's global research with Ipsos MORI revealed that one in five young people have given up hope that we can fix the climate – because 62 per cent say they see much more about the problem than its solutions (Futerra and Ipsos MORI, 2021).

That fatalism is the enemy of action. Today's tragedy of climate change, with the moral that man is the real monster, is so narratively satisfying it's become dangerously believable. For many traditional environmentalists, giving up this story would be a wrench. Even those who understand the dangerous psychology of fatalism struggle with their own addiction to the 'it's all our own fault, and we deserve what's coming' narrative.

Let's flip the script.

This is an adventure. Climate action and solutions are an epic quest, with unexpected twists, huge stakes and, if we get it right, a happy ending. That's the story I've spent decades working out how to tell: cutting out the guilt and dodging around the fear in most climate messaging to the heart-pounding excitement of the journey we're on.

This is the new narrative we desperately need, of overcoming the odds rather than being overwhelmed by them. We need swashbuckling daring, bravery and courage, guile and desperate invention, unlikely friendships and alliances forged in fire.

That's the Solutionist story.

Storytelling as Solutionists

I've learnt a few things about what works for brands, businesses, activists and leaders in telling this story. I've organized my advice in this chapter under two headings, Marketing and Movements, because you might be selling a product and/or service or you might be trying to lead social change. Many of the communications tools are equally applicable to both, but there are nuances between them.

Before we dig into those proven tactics there's one thing that's always the first priority, whether you're marketing or movement making: you must know your audience.

Bricks, Golds and Greens

There are so many audience typologies available when you start planning a communication or marketing campaign. Most are based on demographics – age, gender, politics, geography and so on. When planning messages, I've found one of those audience segmentations to be mind-blowingly accurate and an excellent discipline for testing your own assumptions about what might work.

The 'values modes' approach was developed by Pat Dade, a wonderful American partial to bear hugs and loud laughs. Instead of demographics, it's based upon detailed psychographics. That means rather than segmenting audiences by gender or age, it reveals the impact that our values have on how we receive any message.

Pat spent decades honing the scientific underpinning to this Values Modes Typology, and he named the three typologies he discovered as Pioneers, Prospectors and Settlers. I use his insights every day, but I kept getting his official names of the groups mixed up, so Pat gave me permission to rename them Brick, Gold and Green.

This is a typology for entire populations. In my experience, Solutionists might weight a 'little' towards the Green type, although not exclusively. I could have drawn a complicated matrix of Bricks, Golds and Greens aligned against Architects, Accelerators and Actioners, but honestly, there's folks who fit in every box of that matrix. The three 'A's are about leadership style, this communications typology is about messaging to audiences.

The Gold/Prospector type is the largest segment, usually 40–60 per cent of any population, with Green/Pioneer as 20–40 per cent and Brick/Settler the smallest at 20–30 per cent. Depending on where in the world you are, those scales can change. You're always more likely to meet Gold types than the others:

- The Greens – Greens live in a 'big' world, always interested in and concerned about news from everywhere.

They feel more connected to 'communities of interest' who care about the same things rather than geographically based communities. Local issues pale in comparison to global challenges for Greens. They seek change, love asking new questions, and the more novel the solution, the better. Psychologically they are designated as 'inner directed', which means their personal ethics matter more to them than other people's opinion. They love thinking about the future and mistrust tradition. Once a topic, product or movement is 'mainstream', the Greens tend to lose interest, or even dismiss it.

- The Bricks – Bricks put their family and home at the centre of their world. International issues and concerns are almost mythological for them; local is everything. They prefer things to be 'normal' and are suspicious of the 'latest fad' – assuming it's cover for poor practice. They are particularly wary of crime and support punishment for wrongdoing. Also 'inner directed', their ethics matter most to them, rather than society's opinion. Diametrically opposite to the Greens, they respect tradition and caring for the community as high virtues. Thinking about the future makes them anxious and they are slow to adopt social changes. If a topic, product or movement has 'stood the test of time', they'll accept it.

- The Golds – Distinct from the other two groups, Golds are 'outer-directed' personalities, so they are primarily motivated by what others think of them. Their world view is neither global like the Greens nor local like the Bricks; a Gold's world is themselves. The promise of success excites them, and they welcome opportunities to show their abilities and enjoy looking good. They follow fashions, love celebrities and seek new ideas and novel experiences. They are optimistic about the future and search for opportunities and advancements. If a topic, product or movement is mainstream and socially 'desirable', they are in.

Remember, these aren't demographics (Bricks aren't likely to be older, and there are equal numbers of male/female Golds). For example, many CEOs and politicians are Golds, because ambition for power and recognition tends to be driven by 'outer-directed' personality traits.

The first rule of effective communication is always: everyone isn't you. If you're a Green trying to sell a product to Golds, don't be surprised if your earnest entreaties to buy the product to 'save the planet' don't work. Golds plastering 'new' and 'as worn by celebrities' over everything won't connect with Greens or Bricks. And Bricks shouldn't be shocked when Greens or Golds want to upend social traditions. In the Solutions Starters box for this chapter I'll set out some tactics for using this typology when developing messages.

If you're like me, then you'll see some parts of yourself in all three (I'm a Green who adores new shoes in a very Gold way). Or you might be amazed that everyone isn't your type. When I work with teams on this segmentation, people are astonished that others in their team are happy to admit they belong to a different segment. The Green type especially can be shocked that other people proudly claim to be a Brick or a Gold. Another way to see these three are as 'archetypes'. We all meet these people in our lives, and we weave these personalities into our stories. They all take important roles and balance each other out. There are Green

Solutionists, Brick Solutionists and Gold Solutionists – and we need them all. Plan your messages to include everyone.

Marketing solutions

Your solution might be a product, service, experience, event or other 'commercial' action that you need people to buy into. Indeed, your first audience might be your own colleagues and staff.

There are success strategies (and pitfalls to avoid) that every Solutionist should know when trying to sell sustainability.

Who is the hero?

When we're communicating sustainability solutions, it's easy to forget the first rule of marketing: consumer first.

All too often, when brands or businesses first dip a toe into purpose or sustainability comms, marketing teams fall into the trap of thinking the company is the hero. They describe what 'we are proud to have achieved' and how 'we are doing more than X competitor'. All too often my agency Futerra is sent marketing briefs asking us to help brands 'take more credit for what we're doing' or 'make better sustainability claims'. They forget that this is utterly irrelevant to their customer, who wants to know what your product's sustainability means for them.

I can't state this bluntly enough: no one is interested in your sustainability claims. Consumers only, utterly and always, want to know how your solution is going to make them:

- feel better about their personal environmental impact (not yours);
- help them make the world a better place (not hear how you're doing that);
- believe that the solution works better/is cheaper/has special powers for them, because it's sustainable (but not that they have to sacrifice to be sustainable).

When you're telling the story of your business's sustainability, you aren't the hero – your consumer is. She is the protagonist, the Dorothy in Oz or the Luke Skywalker. He is looking for a guide, his Good Witch of the West or Obi Wan Kenobi. They want your support, but they are not getting it. Instead, all too often, you're stuffing claims about your own effort down their throat, and wondering why your 'sustainability marketing' isn't working.

Futerra asked consumers in the UK and the United States what they actually wanted from you. The vast majority (88%) say they want brands to help them lead a more sustainable lifestyle, but 43 per cent say that brands are doing the opposite, making it harder for them to be environmentally friendly and ethical in their daily life.

Help make your consumer feel like a hero, and they'll reward you for it.

Honesty always

We're all familiar with the idea that consumers – particularly Millennials, those born between 1981 and 1996 – are seeking out brands with purpose.

Gen Z – the newest generation to enter the marketplace and the workforce, born between 1997 and 2012 – are also looking for brands to make a difference. They are seeking something more than purpose: they are seeking honesty. Because while Gen Z have the same heart, the same spirit of sustainability, as their predecessors, they also bring an added dash of distrust.

Futerra, in partnership with the Consumer Goods Forum, commissioned research into this group and found that most Gen Z consumers think big brands are dishonest about all sustainability issues – from treatment of workers to climate impacts (2019). Raised online and in a hyper-consumerist society that faces ever more urgent crises, this is a generation that is ready to take matters into their own hands. So, rather than ask brands to tell them their purpose and assume those brands are taking meaningful action, Gen Z are saying: tell me what you're doing, and I'll decide if it's good enough. Evidence is everything.

This means exposing your progress – or not – on sustainability for all to see. There are lots of ways to pull back the curtains on your product or service, all of them meaningful:

- *Publish progress.* Communicate your policy and your performance (not just your purpose). This means longer- and shorter-term goals, an action plan, and what you've achieved so far. It also means being open about the problems and unmet goals along the way. This is the first step to making meaningful strides on sustainability and many brands already publish this kind of information – make sure yours is one of them.
- *Transparent pricing.* Show a cost breakdown, so consumers can see what they're paying for. Sancho's, a

UK-based ethical fashion retailer, offers tiered pricing options that explicitly cover different parts of the product's production, marketing and other overheads. They explain why on their website: 'The truth is sustainable fashion costs more to make, being open about this allows customers to make a choice about how much they are willing to pay.'

- *Traceability.* Make your ingredients or materials fully traceable, so your customers can see the reality behind your shiny final product. Use something like Storybird's digital app, which can guide your consumers along your product's full supply chain journey, from raw materials to store shelf, just by scanning a QR code.
- *Hard numbers.* State the real-terms sustainability of your product on its packaging: the amount of water it has used, the carbon it has emitted, the airmiles it has travelled. A growing number of brands are embracing this kind of on-product data, from Adidas and Allbirds to Oatly and Wahaca.

Of course, the truth is rarely perfect. Thankfully, that's not what Gen Z are expecting; they just want to know they're not being lied to. In fact, disclosing failures is a helpful step towards showing the sincerity consumers are seeking. Nearly half (45 per cent) of Gen Z say they would trust a brand more if they were honest about a sustainability challenge with their product, and just 13 per cent would trust it less (Futerra, 2019).

So, get ready to wear your sustainability progress on your sleeve, say sorry for mistakes if (when!) they happen, and focus on how to do better. Your journey towards sustainability is more important to today's consumers than any polished purpose statement.

Grievous greenwashing

Just because your intentions are pure doesn't mean you're immune to greenwashing. Too often Solutionists believe that their strong purpose protects them from being misleading in their marketing – it doesn't.

That's because most businesses rarely set out with the malicious intent to greenwash – a term that is defined as '[making] people believe that your company is doing more to protect the environment than it really is'. More often than not, greenwashing is the product of good intentions, an enthusiastic desire to share what you've done well. That doesn't excuse it, but it helps you to know what to look out for in your own communications.

Some of the most common ways to inadvertently greenwash include:

- Vague language and fluffy terms. These are words that sound good but don't mean much, like 'eco-friendly', 'biodegradable' and 'sustainable'.
- Using 'green' imagery. Pictures of trees and meadows in your branding can create the illusion of sustainability without offering any real evidence. If you're showing something visually, be sure you can back it up.
- Long words and technical jargon. Your claims should be backed by science, but not need a science degree to make sense of. Your job is to make your sustainability credentials easy for your customer to understand.
- No proof. Any claims you make need evidence – and

that evidence should be easy to find even if it makes your message 'wordy'.
- Being the 'best' of a bad bunch. Claiming to be better than others means little if the comparison is with businesses doing little to support the environment.
- Disproportionate claims. If one aspect of your product is 'green' but the other 90 per cent of its ingredients or processes are harmful, shouting about how environmentally friendly it is will be misleading.

The science of sustainability can be complex, and it's easy to over-simplify. The best way to avoid the trap of greenwashing – however innocent your purpose – is to work with people who understand the technicalities and the rules. This will also give you the confidence you need to steer clear of greenwash's close cousin: greenhush.

Greenhushing happens

If you weren't already worried about greenwashing, the section above might have made you jittery about it. You're not alone. Greenwashing can harm your reputation and increasingly comes with legal consequences. In early 2022, the UK's Competition and Markets Authority conducted a thorough review of companies' claims, and the European Commission previously found 42 per cent of claims to be greenwash (European Commission, 2021). There's good reason to be careful – but it is equally harmful to say nothing at all.

Greenhush is just that: staying silent on your ethical and environmental commitments and achievements. Keeping your head below the parapet is safe, and it avoids any risk of controversy. It also comes at a cost to the sustainability movement more broadly.

First, greenhush means that no one can see your solutions credentials – and that means no one can review or give you feedback on them. Your stakeholders and customers, as well as activists and analysts, deserve transparency from any business.

Second, words help actions speak louder. While being 'all talk, no action' is one of the most common problems identified by the sustainability movement, the opposite is also true. Enacting robust climate policies that could set an example or provide a blueprint for others is a missed opportunity if it's not shouted from the rooftops. Telling the world what you're doing is an important form of advocacy – don't underestimate this.

Finally, greenhush can silently support a myth we have already met: 'sustainability as a cost centre'. Because without offering your consumer the chance to be a sustainability hero, you won't get any of the benefits. Customers can't reward you for it with their preference and loyalty, and investors can't prioritize you. The result is that your sustainability activity is a burden, undermining its place in your organization and in others.

Jesper Brodin of IKEA is afraid of brands' silence on sustainability: 'If you're silent, then there is no dialogue, and that is a disaster. As brands, we have the privilege where our communications can actually influence things. We must transparently share what we have done, what we are doing and what we can't yet do – where we are stuck. That's how we start a dialogue that can change things.'

Big-up benefits

Often, wannabe-Solutionists cite what they see as the biggest barrier to selling their solution: the value–action gap. This is the idea that consumers typically tell them in focus groups and surveys that they want more sustainable options – then when offered them, they don't buy them. This is one of the biggest and most dangerous myths in sustainability. In reality, the problem is not with consumers' inconsistency, but with the product you're selling.

Sustainability alone is not a big enough benefit. Consumers do want to be the hero and buy more sustainable products, but they also want to buy products that are delicious, fun, attractive, cheap, good-quality, useful and easy to use. Offer them something that's better for the planet but falls apart, tastes bad or feels boring, and you haven't fulfilled the brief.

Sustainability should offer your customer more. Do your carefully sourced ingredients taste better? Are your ethically made clothes longer lasting and better looking? And what barriers does it remove – does it make refillable packaging the easiest choice, or plant-based plastic the cheapest? This is the value you must sell.

Think about Smol, whose plastic-free laundry tablets are a similar price to the supermarket standard while being automatically delivered when you need them – and leave your laundry fresher. As they put it, 'eco-effective cleaning with convenience that's affordable'. Or Green Toys, who emphasize the safety of their 100 per cent recycled toys – 'it's #1', their website says – above their environmental credentials. Allbirds describe their alternative materials as much in terms of comfort as sustainability: their shoes are 'light and breezy', made from 'cushiony' sugarcane.

Go beyond guilt-busting feel-good offerings and tell your customer how sustainability has upgraded your product in more ways than one. This banishes the sustainability marketer's enemy: worthiness. And above all, it makes sure you've answered any consumer's biggest question: 'What's in it for me?'

Solutions movements

So much for selling products, but what about selling change? Many Solutionists reading this might not have a product or service to sell; instead they have a new vision of the world, a behaviour or a community to uplift. That's not marketing, it's movement making.

Building a movement means finding a crowd of people who share your beliefs and galvanizing that energy with an exciting plan of action. Much of my advice above still stands, especially the Brick, Green, Gold audience typology. But movements do need a different activation strategy to ignite change.

At Futerra, after working with, and researching, movements across the world, we found a formula for those that worked:

People + Passion × Plot = Change

Driving change involves these three (helpfully alliterative) ingredients: people, passion and plot. You need a huge crowd of excited, passionate people who arrive in their droves (25 per cent, preferably) and are willing to take action. Then, you need a plan of action – a journey plotted on a map that will get you, and your crowd, to your solutions destination.

We can see this equation play out in any of history's great movements. The civil rights movement gave millions of African Americans with a deep sense of injustice a clear, ambitious and concrete goal: the end of legal segregation. And the rise of vegetarianism involved millions of people, with a strongly held desire to eat in a way that respected human, animal and planetary health, rallying around one simple action: eat plants.

In a world of likes and follows, it's easy to get hung up on the 'people' part of the recipe. Growing a following is a challenge in itself, let alone finding the passionate, proactive kindred spirits that will make action possible. Once you've got it, it's tempting to think you've done the hard part. Now you've got friends and followers, you've hit the 'quarter rule' of the crowd behind you – where will you lead them?

That little multiplication sign before 'Plot' is there for a reason. It is only once passionate people take action that change can happen. When they do – that's when the world can change. In my career, I've met thousands of Solutionists. Their goals and their starting points vary, though they are all determined to make good things happen. The most common thing that holds many of them back? Not having a clear 'plot'.

Ultimately, your plot will depend on your goal and your people. Every Solutionist will chart a different course. There are factors you should consider that will help you draw your map and plot your next steps.

How can you start easily? The plot of any good story has an arc, with small events reaching a crescendo. Get people involved in a simple action, to build momentum towards bigger change. Get to know your followers, to best understand what's most doable for them. Build your next steps from there.

Who else should come with you? Before any plot really unfolds, we meet all the key characters involved. Who could really shape your journey? This could be an experienced mentor, an academic in a specific field, a young person with a fresh perspective. Always think about how people with lived experience can be at the centre of the action, in ways that avoid burdening them with emotional labour.

How should you spend your budget and plan your time-line? Most plots cost money and take time. Once you can see your end goal and the steps needed to get there, you can see where and when time and money are most needed. Depending on your plan, you might decide to invest up front in what's needed to get to the final stages, or do your first steps on a shoestring to save funds for later.

Being a Solutionist isn't the easy road, and nowhere is this truer than when it comes to identifying the plot for a movement. And as with every aspect of your sustainability journey, it must come from a place of authenticity. Action for action's sake will ring hollow. Picture your vision and make it the most beautiful of possibilities – then trust that you can tell the story that will get you there.

EXERCISE   Solutions starters

The Brick, Gold, Green typology gives you a wonderful window to look at your 'ask' or call-to-action in your marketing or movement:

1   Try writing out your message in a way that would appeal to each. Even if you're only targeting one type, the exercise will reveal angles and ideas you might otherwise not have seen. It will also counteract any bias you have towards messages to which you personally respond.

2   Then, plot out who the perfect 'messenger' for your solution would be, again for each type.

3   For Bricks, they will be trusted local leaders and even family members, respected authorities, beloved faces (such as David Attenborough) and those who exude safety and savings.

4   For Greens, vocal and authentic activists will be listened to, as well as creatives, inventors and artists. Experts and academics can resonate as long as they aren't too 'mainstream'.

5   For Golds, start with celebrities – famous footballers, TV and film stars, style gurus – anyone famous with their hand on the pulse of modern culture. The more recognized, the better.

This will help you identify unlikely or unexpected supporters or spokespeople for your solution.

And remember, we need campaigns that reach all these groups. It will take everyone to change everything.

CHAPTER NINE

Myths and traps

Having worked with Solutionists for over 20 years, I've seen how every business embarking or progressing on its sustainability journey can find itself in a maze. Wrong turns and dead-ends abound. Mistakes are repeated and leaders feel lost. The most frustrating thing about this maze? It's often of Solutionists' own making.

It is made up of a multitude of wrong thinking. Past experience, human bias, fears, assumptions and pride line the pathways of the solutions maze, sending well-meaning Solutionists on a needlessly complicated series of lefts and rights (and wrongs).

The interesting – and helpful – thing about these misguided ideas is that they aren't unique to any one person, business or problem. They are repeated time and again by business leaders and changemakers from all sorts of industries and business sizes. I've made every single one of these mistakes myself, over and over again, until I finally made a map of the maze – with myths and traps marked upon it.

Some of these we've already mentioned in passing, but they are so common I want to throw extra light on them here!

The myths

Myth 1: It's all too late

Every day there's another horrible story: a flood, fire or storm, an outrage or act of injustice. Headlines about 'uninhabitable Earth' and 'social breakdown' are unrelenting and overwhelming. For too many people, it's also a sign that nothing can be done anymore.

We must remember that all these doom-laden articles and social media posts are opinions, not prophesies. They garner attention not because they are correct, but because they are click-bait.

I asked Johanna Chao Kreilick, President of the Union of Concerned Scientists (a group of over 250 experts in climate and social science), are we doomed? She told me that

> it's not too late to make a difference. The science tells us that limiting the worst climate change impacts requires wholesale societal shifts away from fossil fuels and widespread global action to slash heat-trapping emissions by ramping up energy efficiency, renewable energy and battery storage; modernizing electric grids; electrifying vehicles, buildings and

industry; and increasing public transit options. If done well, such investments can address long-standing environmental injustices and create good-paying jobs.

This is the nuance we don't hear in the media. The threat is huge and growing worse by the day, and there are impacts baked in that we must adapt to and protect the most vulnerable people and places from. Things need to change, a lot. But nothing in the climate science prevents us from doing something about it.

Our attitude counts. Futerra's Solutionist Survey conducted with Ipsos MORI in over 23 countries revealed that 58 per cent of the global population are either very or somewhat optimistic about our chances of tackling climate change (Futerra and Ipsos MORI, 2021). However, 31 per cent were pessimistic or even fatalistic about that chance. Compare that to the Solutionists I surveyed, where 70 per cent counted as optimistic and only 2 per cent as at all pessimistic.

What do Solutionists know that makes them so much more positive about our chances? They know that something can be done, because they are doing it. The very best antidote to fatalism is action.

Myth 2: Sustainability is a duty, not a benefit

The myth of sustainability as a burden goes beyond just cost. It is often seen as an obligation, a cross to bear for those businesses 'considerate' enough to bother with it. It is seen as worthy, and worse – boring.

This framing of sustainability puts it in the realm of responsibility and duty, instead of opportunity. What do we do with onerous obligations? Just enough to fulfil them. Most people tick the box and move on to something more fun.

A feeling of responsibility is not conducive to feelings of enthusiasm – and enthusiasm is what sustainability deserves. Solutions can make customers fall in love with you and bring new investors on board. It's your chance to engage your colleagues in new ways and come up with original ideas that will excite you, them and the world.

Remember Chapter 1 on the Solutions Economy: this is a trillion-dollar opportunity, not a duty.

Myth 3: 'We're already doing enough'

I hear this everywhere, and it's an easy trap to fall into. So many businesses and brands want 'credit for what we've already done'.

Too often, doing something feels like doing enough. It's simply not – neither in the eyes of experts nor, more importantly, in the eyes of your consumers.

Consumers' bar for 'enough' is higher than you think. More than two-thirds (68 per cent) of US consumers say that in order to feel comfortable buying from a brand, they expect it to be clear about its values and to take a stand on them (Kantar, 2020). And 59 per cent of adults are 'disappointed' in big-name brands that still haven't got their sustainability initiatives right (SWNS Media Group, 2021). In a world of worsening environmental crisis and social inequity, just taking credit for what you've already done isn't going to work – because compared to the problem, it looks inadequate.

What does enough look like? It's stating what your business believes in and making sure every action you take is aligned behind it, every time and everywhere. It's creating new solutions that tackle both climate and justice. It's going above and beyond, and showing as well as telling.

The traps

Trap 1: Trying to be perfect

We've all heard the saying: 'perfect is the enemy of good'. This might not be true in other areas of business, where reaching maximum performance and 100 per cent guarantees are the standard. But when it comes to sustainability, requiring perfection risks outright failure.

Solutions don't need to be perfect. Indeed, complete sustainability has not yet been achieved by any business. Ethical and environmental transformation is a process, and a series of improvements that show intention, commitment and ambition.

For many years, my friend Hannah Jones led Nike's sustainability endeavours. Instead of waiting to be perfect, she set huge goals and radical transparency about what wasn't perfect yet (far from it) and what Nike was going to do about it. Corporate Responsibility and Impact Reports on Nike's website reach back to 2001. Even today, after years of improving their business practices, their sustainability plans are called 'Move to Zero'. The movement is as important as the destination.

Sometimes, you might even need a little help along the road. Striving for perfect can be isolating and cause blind spots to build up. Abby Maxman, President and CEO of Oxfam America, has this advice for us: 'Never hesitate to ask for help and see feedback as a gift.'

Trap 2: Failing to focus

When it comes to your business's sustainability, there's housekeeping that any company needs to stay on top of – using recycled paper, limiting water waste, cutting down your electricity bill. Then, depending on what your business does, there are areas where your material impact will be far greater than others. These are the areas that deserve your focus, because these actions will multiply your positive impact – it's where your solutions will be found.

Identifying those 'big tickets' could take some lateral thinking, because the most obvious areas might not always be the most impactful. Take creative advertising and marketing agencies as an example. If we go beyond recyclable coffee cups and switching the lights off, we might think of business flights to meet international clients perhaps, or even the carbon footprint of the server used to store terabytes of data-heavy design files. A creative agency could focus on these activities, scrabbling around to shave a fraction of a carbon emission here and there – but the area that really deserves their focus could reduce their material impact tenfold. Namely, their client list. If a creative agency is working with a fossil-fuel company, they are helping that company to multiply its activities – and therefore its harm. This is the agency's 'brainprint', and it dwarfs their 'footprint'. That's why Futerra pioneered Client Disclosure Reports for professional services companies. Agencies and advisory consultancies reveal their turnover as a pie-chart, with each slice showing the industries they work for. That allows other sustainability-focused clients to decide what company they want to keep.

Where is your business's most significant material impact on people and planet? Think big, then zoom out even further. It might be somewhere that isn't comfortable to think about, but truly your biggest impact.

Trap 3: Not bringing people with you

Ten years ago, every employee of Unilever Australia arrived at work to find themselves with a brand-new job title: Head of Sustainability. Everyone from the sales team to the lab technicians was issued a new, personalized business card and a 'job manual' explaining Unilever's business case for sustainability.

Unilever has come to be something of a gold standard when it comes to corporate sustainability, and a big part of that success comes from their ability to bring everyone in their business with them. Sustainability is not just the remit of a specific 'impact' department that works in a silo. People in roles across your business are often the ones best placed to see how the sustainability of their work under their remit could be improved. Often, they just need the confidence to share their sustainability idea or raise the topic for discussion.

This needn't require everyone in your business to become a sustainability expert overnight. Rather, it's a case of giving everyone the information they need in an accessible way – no jargon, no densely written scientific handouts, just straightforward summaries designed for the layperson. Use stories to explain data and share plenty of examples of what works and what doesn't. Make big ideas concrete and offer inspiration for your teams to imagine what's possible.

Trap 4: Co-opitition

In the survey, and my interviews, I pushed Solutionists to answer the question: What would you most like others working in sustainability to change about how they operate? The answers about what needs to change were a little too consistent for comfort.

Siddharth Sharma, Group Chief Sustainability Officer at Tata Sons, said we must 'collaborate and look beyond the confines of our immediate jobs'. Steve Waygood, Chief Responsible Investment Officer at Aviva Investors, was more forthright about the problem: 'Ego. Some is healthy. But too much leads to infighting.' Amanda Gardiner, Head of Sustainability Innovation and Engagement at Meta put it simply: 'Remember that sustainability is a team sport, and we have to collaborate to get it done!' And Jon Khoo, Head of Sustainability (EAAA) at Interface, doubled down on the ego problem: 'I think there's a need to take the "ego" out of sustainability and environmentalism. For too long we've looked for a saviour… moreover someone with a good idea/approach has sought to "own" a solution (it's a hero-centric view). The reality is that without the teams behind them and the spirit of collaboration – they would never have succeeded.'

Tata, Aviva Investors, Meta and Interface are in very different industries, but their sustainability leaders are all experiencing the same thing within the Solutionist community: too much intellectual competitiveness.

Perhaps there's a reason for that. In the Introduction I mentioned that one of the most significant benefits of being a Solutionist is that it's fascinating and intellectually thrilling.

Far too easily, that excitement about ideas can turn into competition over them. That leads to infighting and one-upmanship. What can we do about this? First, acknowledge that while we value cooperation in theory, Solutionists often default to competition in reality. Let's accept it doesn't always come easily and make conscious, concerted efforts to collaborate and recognize that it will take hard work. Because we're all smart enough to know that we will only solve this, together.

Nigel Topping has more experience of this than most. In 2020, he was named the UN Climate Change High-Level Champion for COP26 in Glasgow. That entailed wrangling thousands of businesses, and just as many politicians and civil servants, around making commitments for the business sector at the giant climate conference. When I asked him what Solutionists need to change about how they operate, he didn't hold back: 'Resist falling into the Monty Python's Life of Brian "splitters" trap. Take time to appreciate the unique gifts of fellow mission-driven organizations, double down on commitment to mission first, organization second, self last, and collaborate, radically!' He also pushed us to reach beyond our comfort zones: 'Don't demonize the guardians of the status quo, find a way to engage with them as humans.'

Challenges like climate change and human rights are big, and they're systemic. Achieving the change needed to really move the needle requires shifts happening across whole industries and entire countries.

The biggest leaders in sustainability also know that sharing is central to their success. Understanding that the need for industry-wide change was more important than their own performance alone, multinational fashion company Kering made their sustainability tool open-source. They developed an app in 2016 called My EP&L (Environmental Profit & Loss account), which works out the environmental impact of specific fashion products along their supply chain – and they made it available for other companies to use (Chen, 2018). After all, keeping it a secret would only limit the good it could do.

There will always be areas where your business's competitive spirit can thrive – you can tell your story in the most compelling way and offer products that are uniquely exciting. Doing sustainability properly means making collaboration second nature. Join coalitions that put you in the same room as your industry peers to tackle problems together. Offer help and ask for it. Even – and especially – from your competitors.

Now that you're armed with knowledge of the myths and traps that lie awaiting you, you've got a much better chance of navigating the maze. Keep them in mind as you take your next steps, and you'll find your route far less convoluted – and a lot more fun.

EXERCISE   Solutions starters

I like to make a 'traps map' when I start a project.

  I'll create my beautiful solutions plan (for me, that usually means a long PowerPoint). It will be well thought through and complete.

Then I'll sleep on it, come back the next day, and try to look at the plan as if I were my worst critic. How many ways can I think of to screw this up? What scenarios, both sensible and fantastical, might derail the plan? Can I think of any cautionary tales of projects like mine that didn't work?

For even better results, I'll invite colleagues and friends to come play 'bad cop' on the project and identify every flaw, oversight and possible trap laid within it. It's quite fun.

A plan isn't final until it's been through the process, either in my head or with help. Never have I created something that came through unchanged. And my solutions are the better for it.

CHAPTER TEN

Joyful entrepreneurship

You can only drive the change you want to see in the world if you're taking care of yourself. And that's not always easy, but it's something that I come back to. I try to have good daily routines. I meditate first thing in the morning when I wake up. I try to go for a walk in the woods, even if it's only for 20 minutes, every morning if I can. That really grounds me in myself, but also in my purpose. Like this morning, I worried I was going to be late for this interview, so I chugged out the door and took a 20-minute walk in the redwoods, and I still got to one of my favourite trees, and I put my hand on it and looked up in the branches, for a moment. Those small things for me are really powerful and really important for staying grounded and showing up as the best person, leader and mom I can be. KATE BRANDT, CSO OF GOOGLE

First the good news. Despite its challenges, working on sustainability really is a game with no losers. The world gets a little bit better – a little healthier, a little more beautiful, a little more just and free – and you get to enjoy what it feels like to have made that difference.

Study after study has shown that doing good for others does just as much good for you. Helping other people can decrease symptoms of depression, and volunteering actively improves wellbeing. Being denied the opportunity to help another person lowers our mood, indicating that offering kindness to others may even be a basic psychological human need. And the 'helper's high' really is a thing: neuroimaging has shown that donating money to charity engages the brain's reward system in just the same way as when money is received. Recent research has shown that even helping a robot can improve our mood. Whatever the news and social media might have us believe, science tells us that we are hardwired to do good – and our brains reward us for it.

These personal benefits are ones that today's working population sorely needs. Wellbeing and engagement at work go hand in hand, with high engagement linked to low levels of burnout. Stress and burnout reached an all-time high in the United States in 2021, and a global study has shown that Australia leads the world in rates of burnout – at least 61 per cent of Australian workers say they are feeling at least somewhat burnt-out (McKinsey & Company, 2021). When it comes to satisfaction at work, Japan and Hong Kong trail behind other countries, with 51 per cent of workers in both countries saying they are not satisfied with their job (Randstad, 2019). And according to a US study of workplace happiness, nearly two in five people (38%) are not happy in their job (Indeed, 2021).

These numbers paint a picture of a world that is, by all accounts, pretty unhappy at work. Nevertheless, 96 per cent of unhappy workers in the United States believe that happiness is still possible for them (Indeed, 2021). The solution, you may not be surprised to hear, is to become a Solutionist.

Given what we know about the mood-boosting benefits of doing good, it's not surprising to hear that it plays a part in how we feel about our jobs. In one UK study, employees were asked about 12 different factors that contribute to wellbeing at work – including fair pay, achievement and flexibility. The winners were 'feeling energized', 'having a sense of belonging' and, you guessed it, 'feeling a sense of purpose'.

Purpose is a complex concept, but workers describe it as including their understanding of how they impact the bigger picture and believing that their work makes the world a better place.

Connecting with a sense of purpose at work has all kinds of benefits, like making people more likely to stay in their job. Research with employees in the United States has shown that a sense of purpose boosts feelings of connection, pride and achievement in work. Outside work, it prompts people to feel more energized, resilient and healthy. People with a sense of purpose even experience lower levels of mortality. Do good, be happy, live longer – pretty compelling, no? The bad news is, it doesn't always feel that way for Solutionists.

We might be wired to make the world a better place but staying positive doesn't always come naturally – especially after too many late nights in the office or in the face of a daunting deadline. Orienting ourselves to the problems we're solving in a positive, self-sustaining way is essential if we are to – as this chapter's title suggests – enjoy it. And the solutions we're creating are utterly dependent on that enjoyment.

So, how can we fully engage with the problem at hand – whether it's a terrifying climate crisis, disturbing human rights injustices, or any of the overwhelming problems in between – while also steering clear of doom-laden thinking? And what about the challenge of navigating the denials and pushbacks of those whose heads are firmly in the sand?

The nature of any kind of changemaking requires you to swim upstream. You are doing something different and difficult, and face resistance in its many forms. Whether you're in a role that means you're driving change within a large corporate, the founder of a sustainable business, a social change thought-leader or an on-the-ground activist, you will likely experience many of the stressors that can lead to burnout.

'Hustle culture', with its #thankgoditsmonday hashtags and 'hustle harder' office slogans, has become a pervasive force in today's workplaces. It can be difficult for anyone to resist these sorts of norms, but when your work is geared towards making things better for people or the planet, deciding to rest instead of grind can be guilt-inducing. Combine this with 24/7 news cycles and the infinite scroll of social media spotlighting the scale and urgency of the world's problems, and the Solutionists trying to turn the tide find themselves in a perfect storm of exhaustion and pressure.

Today's changemakers are in danger of becoming a burnt-out generation. In a global study of young change-makers, just 7 per cent reported experiencing no symptoms of burnout since starting work on their social entrepreneur-ship project (Ioan, 2021). Working on the world's biggest problems – in any context – can leave people exhausted physically, mentally and emotionally. Your sleep is affected, and low moods can descend upon you. Being burnt-out also feeds cynicism and self-doubt.

This is bad news for the burnt-out, whose mental health and home life fall victim to their passion and drive to make a difference in the wider world. It is also detrimental to the very work Solutionists are sacrificing themselves for. When Solutionists suffer, so do the solutions they are trying to create.

I was both honoured and not a little surprised when the CEOs I spoke with for the book confided such honest stories of their own struggles to cope. For example, Mads Nipper shared:

> When things look difficult and even gloomy, it just usually fuels my motivation to do everything I possibly can. So, the bigger risk is that I end up being almost burning too much for the issue and then saying, 'How can I cope with that?' Because, if we fill up our mental and our physical capacity with everything that's so important, then when more urgencies hit, and they do all the time, whether it is really poor business numbers or a crisis or whatever, it fills you up to here. I've had instances of this, and I choose to share

them very openly in my organization. Over Easter this year, I was fully loaded already and then we ran into a really tough short-term financial crisis. I worked through it, but then on the weekend, I just physically got ill. It was only 24 hours, but my body told me, 'No more.' That was a realization, saying, 'I can't fill myself up 110 per cent all the time.' I also chose to share that with my thousands of colleagues, because they're seeing it happens to me and I'm sure it happens to some of you, but let's take care, because we are not the best version of ourselves if that happens.

In an international study with social changemakers – including social entrepreneurs, activists, impact-investors and those working in non-profits – addressing burnout was found not only to have benefits for personal wellbeing, but for building more collaborative relationships. And when changemakers took part in an 18-month programme to support their wellbeing, they reported their leadership style becoming more supportive and their overall approach to collaboration becoming more open. Addressing burnout and boosting wellbeing is a win–win–win – for you, your team and your mission.

So, how can you prevent burnout? How can you rest when your goals are meaningful and urgent? How can you recharge when there aren't enough hours in the day?

The following are tactics drawn from research on stress-reduction, my own survival tactics after decades in the field and practical examples that Solutionists shared with me through interviews and surveys for this book.

Joy for its own sake

You're allowed to be happy, to rest and to enjoy yourself. Not because doing so will make you a better Solutionist. Not because you need to 'rest the machine' to keep it running. Not taking time today in order to work harder tomorrow. Simply because you are a human being, and joy is part of the package.

Over decades of working with Solutionists I've heard people encouraging each other to slow down and take care of themselves because 'you'll come back stronger', so a holiday 'can give perspective on your next steps', or spending time in nature will 'remind you why we're doing this'. Rest, joy, hobbies and holidays all seen only in relation to improving work performance.

Even worse is when Solutionists earnestly apologize for their own downtime, as if they might be criticized or thought of as 'letting the side down' for reading a novel rather than an IPCC report, or watching a comedy rather than documentary.

I do this all the time. Ask anyone I work with how many holidays (if I take them at all) I frame as helping me become a better changemaker. Or apologize that I can't make the speech because I 'have' to spend pre-booked time with family or friends. How many times I've had to be walked out of the office by colleagues, quite forcibly, when I'm sick.

I promise I've made every stupid self-sacrificing, martyr to the cause, live for my work, excuse.

Deep breath

Why the fuck are we trying to save humanity, if we don't let ourselves enjoy being humans?

Lily Cole is an activist, author and world-famous celebrity. She is constantly bombarded with asks, issues and pressing demands. I asked her how she copes:

> I do disconnect a lot from it. I think that is partly a coping mechanism and partly, I don't know, a response to life. Disconnect in the sense of I don't want to just be thinking about the doom and gloom and how awful the situation is, every waking minute of the day. So, I make an effort to feed my other interests, whether it's art, or film, or laughing with friends, or being with family and being silly, or dancing. All the other things that make life joyful. I think it's really important to keep all of that, because otherwise, why are we living?

We deserve to be playful, rested, obsessed with our hobbies, happily distracted and indulgent to our loves, relationships and fascinations – even if they don't make us better Solutionists. Even if they make us worse ones. Being messy, fulfilled, wonderful human beings is all this has ever been about.

Set boundaries

A 'martyr complex' is all too common for Solutionists. Who hasn't felt that little thrill of self-righteousness when working till midnight on a solution that might change the world? Yawns worn as medals and exhaustion as a ticker-tape parade.

When you're ambitious and impatient for change, working longer and later can feel tempting. And people who are working towards a goal that matters to them and to the world too often feel that taking time to rest is selfish – that they don't deserve to take time off when others are suffering.

This is a trap. Solutionists can quickly find themselves in the clutches of burnout – and, to add insult to injury, their long hours don't actually mean they're achieving more. Research proves that in any given day, productivity declines after 8 hours and drops quickly after 9 hours (Krumina, 2017). And over the course of a week, productivity falls sharply after 50 hours of work, and stops almost completely after 55 hours (Pencavel, 2014).

Everyone's working style and context will be a little different, so think carefully about the best ways for you to contain your working hours and keep them manageable. This could include:

- tracking your hours worked, and setting an upper limit that you commit to sticking to;
- accepting that you can't do everything, and planning which tasks you can hand off to a colleague or deprioritize;
- letting colleagues know in advance when you won't be available, so they know to get in touch with you before you log off – not two hours into your downtime;
- being ready to say no to new commitments, confident in the knowledge that doing less will better serve you and your mission.

Boundaries can also just be in your head – deciding when to stop thinking about the problems and solutions, let alone working on them. Solutionists or not, we are all human. Stress, fatigue and limited attention spans are a reality for even the most determined and passionate of us. The answer here is to accept your limits and work within them.

Rest wisely

There's no 'right' way to rest, other than the way that best replenishes your energy. For some people, that might involve being horizontal with a favourite box set; for others, it could mean cooking dinner for your kids, or joining a local sewing group or tennis team. While everyone is different, research suggests a couple of ways to spend time that could benefit any of us. Paul Polmon, formally CEO of Unilever, has a very healthy attitude: 'I don't take it all on my shoulders as my own responsibility, I sleep well at night. So, I think always you need to get your oxygen somewhere else. I always worry when people say, "I'm 100% dedicated to Unilever, I work day and night for you." You need to pick up a book, and have friends, and do other things, and I've always tried to do that.'

If you need a little prompting to plan rest (I often do), in my interviews and surveys some restful behaviours came top of many peoples lists.

Spending time in nature is a well-recognized way to relieve stress. The health benefits of forest bathing – spending time in a woodland or forest – have been established scientifically, and thousands of doctors in the United

States, Canada and Scotland have prescribed nature to their patients to relieve stress. As little as 10 minutes in a green space has been found to positively impact psychological and physiological markers of mental wellbeing.

Uyunkar Domingo Peas Nampichkai, indigenous Achuar leader from the Ecuadorian Amazon, told me how he copes with feeling overwhelmed: 'When I'm anxious or overwhelmed, I take deep breaths. I isolate myself close to nature, in the rainforest if I'm there. I take my tobacco (one of their sacred plants) and do a deep analysis on what I've done and what I have to do next.'

Far from the warm Amazon, up in the icy Arctic, renowned glaciologist Dr Twila Moon has almost the same ritual of 'Sinking my hands into clear natural running streams – which has a grounding power that I imagine goes along with bare feet on soft ground.'

Getting creative through art, craft, dance, writing and music has been found to reduce stress and anxiety, restore emotional balance and process negative experiences. The Windcall Institute offers a programme for activist leaders that includes creative pursuits – like journalling, poetry, drawing and sculpture – as a central part of the experience. Nine out of ten participants report that the programme helped them continue their work in a more sustainable way (Windcall Institute, 2009).

Practising mindfulness in activities like meditation, tai chi and yoga is popular and for good reason. Meditation has been found to significantly reduce the experience of stress, depression and burnout after just five weeks. In a study with social justice activists, mindfulness practices effectively healed participants from their burnout experiences and even helped them to become more effective in their work. For Christiana Figueres, the architect of the Paris Agreement, she found deep solace:

> For me, what made a radical difference in my life was to discover a spiritual practice. I'm a student of a Zen Buddhist master who just passed away in January. He was a Vietnamese Zen Buddhist master and his name was Thích Nhất Hạnh. I discovered his teachings in 2013 and I have been a student ever since. And that really was the most radical, I think, not in a negative but in a positive way, the most radical change in my life. So, for me, a spiritual practice is central, which of course includes meditation but goes way beyond that into a daily awareness of who I am and how I turn up in the world, and how I put myself into every interaction that I have.

Moving your body with exercise, dance, yoga or even just a walk is one of the simplest ways to recover your balance, but also too often the first thing we drop when things get busy. Jamie Palmer from Social Supermarket told me: 'The thing which I always regret doing was giving up on fitness. Because it's so easy to do. Going to the gym, it's an hour, and that's an hour I could be working on this big pitch. So, getting back to fitness, that's the number one of what I need to change.'

Be small

Solutionists have a high sense of what psychologists call 'agency' – the sense that you can affect the world around you. While common for Solutionists, this feeling is actually rare in most general populations. Many studies have been conducted on the risks of low agency, feeling powerless and being adrift. However, I couldn't find any on the danger of too much agency – the sense that saving the world sits on your shoulders.

I've felt it. I am educated, belong to a powerful network and have proven to myself I can get things done. Most of the time, that's empowering. Then sometimes, I feel over-whelmed by the responsibility of my choices. What if I spend all this potential in the wrong way? What if there is more impact I could make if I was just smarter/faster/harder-working? I call this 'agency-overwhelm': having the ability to do a lot, but there being too much to do.

Amanda Gardiner, Head of Sustainability Innovation and Engagement at Meta, told me a simple way to think about it: 'You may want to change 100 per cent, but if you can change 1 per cent it's a big deal.' My friend Sarah Corbett, founder of the Craftivist Collective, inspiring gentle protest, reminded me of another way to see this: 'Do it from love, not for love.'

Reminding myself of my smallness, limitations, and that I'm only one of millions of people working to make a difference – that gets me breathing again.

Irma Olguin Jr of Bitwise Industries has a beautiful way to explain it:

> I think it's important for me, I won't speak for anyone else, but for me to recognize that I'm still just one person. I am an imperfect being in many ways, which means that my reach and my influence and my ability to fix only go so far. There are many things that I am not equipped to deal with,

and I have to recognize that I'm not powerful enough for those things. So, not to be overly humble because I'm not attempting to show false humility or anything like that, but some things are beyond me and it's important every day that I know that is true. I still have to be small when I'm standing underneath the sky.

Accept unfinished business

Karimah Hudda, Senior Director of Partnerships and Engagement at Nike, told me how she copes with the stresses of being a Solutionist: 'Learn to live with the fact that the change you are making will manifest long after you have moved on from this job.'

Her point reminded me of how hard it can be to work for change, without knowing if it's working. The problems we Solutionists throw ourselves at are so huge that keeping score against them is impossible, and far too often, it feels like we're losing.

Thankfully, we're not the first Solutionists to face great challenges, and we can look back along the path and see how the impact our predecessors made resonated for generations after their own time. Most of the suffragettes never got to vote. Most early LGBTQIA+ activists never got to marry. Most civil rights activists never saw the first black US President. Inventors of electricity died by candlelight.

These people dedicated their lives for a better future they never lived in. If you're fighting, working, sweating and trying to solve our climate crisis or bend society towards justice, you may never see the better world you're trying to build. That's not how change happens. It happens because people decide to work for better, knowing they may never see it – because they want a life well lived. The reward for action is in the moment of action, not in the world validating that it was worth it.

Professor Heiko Hosomi Spitzeck, Director of the Sustainability Research Center at Fundação Dom Cabral in Brazil, quoted a very apt line from *Rogue One: A Star Wars Story* (2016) to me: 'It doesn't matter if we win, it matters what we fight.'

Give empathy a break

If you've set out to change the world, the chances are your empathy meter regularly maxes out. If you didn't care deeply about injustice and the suffering of others, you likely wouldn't be doing the work you do. Caring is one of your superpowers – but left unchecked, it can become your kryptonite.

Paul Bloom, Professor of Psychology and Cognitive Science at Yale, distinguishes between empathy and compassion. Empathy is, he says, 'feeling the feelings of other people'; while having compassion means 'I give your concern weight, I value it... but I don't necessarily pick up your feelings'. The result is that 'if I have empathy toward you, it will be painful if you're suffering. It will be exhausting... But if I feel compassion for you, I'll be invigorated. I'll be happy and I'll try to make your life better' (Bloom, 2019).

It follows that feeling compassion, rather than immersing yourself in the fullness of empathy, could help prevent what psychologists call 'empathy fatigue'. This type of burnout is characterized by feelings of overwhelm, anger, detachment and, ironically, reduced empathy. Avoiding it takes self-awareness and deliberate steps to challenge your thought process. Step away from empathy and towards compassion:

- Mentally distance yourself from the emotive situation – knowing that this does not mean you don't care about the people suffering, only that you care enough about the problem to take the steps needed to solve it.
- Shift from 'how do you feel?' to 'what do you need?'. Engaging practically with the problem is a sign of compassion instead of empathy and can more easily lead to helpful action.
- Verbalize your feelings. Research has shown that healthcare professionals who described their emotions out loud went on to experience reduced empathic distress three months later. This is likely because naming our emotions can help us acknowledge, process and defuse them.

Multiply wins

When you're trying to make big change happen – particularly if it's institutional or structural – then progress is likely to feel frustratingly slow. Environmental and social progress takes time; it may feel like rolling a boulder, inch by inch, uphill. Wins will seem few and far between, and the disappointments may be many. This is the nature of a Solutionist's work, and one of its more debilitating qualities.

Wins are hidden along your path, if you look for them – they are the milestones along the road to your biggest goal. Break down your ultimate objective into a series of smaller ones, and suddenly you have more to celebrate, and sooner. If your goal is to make sure your organization reaches ambitious carbon reduction targets by 2050, what do you need to achieve in the next two years, even the next six months? Which team members need to be hired? What conversations need to be had? Identify the smallest steps you can take to progress towards your goal. Write a list – the longer, the better. These are your goals now. When you reach one, feel the win – resist the urge to diminish it. Every step is crucial and deserves celebration.

Karina O'Gorman, Head of Force for Good at Innocent Drinks, advised me 'to take it one step at a time. The reality of what needs to be done can be overwhelming, we always seem to feel we are never making a dent in it, so it's crucial to remind yourself you are making progress, however small it might feel'.

Once you've multiplied your wins, it's time to own them. The complex, collective nature of social and environmental change can make achievements feel difficult to attribute to any single person. They are hard to measure, and even harder to attribute to an individual – let alone oneself. Instead of letting this detract from your feelings of success, embrace the joy of collective achievement. Congratulate others and celebrate with them. And know that your contribution was bigger for not being yours alone.

Remember why

You're a Solutionist for a reason. Something made you itch, something pissed you off, something needed fixing.

Sometimes, self-care is as simple as writing 'I'm a Solutionist because...' and then listing, in as simple or complete a way as you like, why you're doing this. It's not always going to be easy, and even with boundaries, rest and help, you're still going to have difficult days. The always forthright Henk Jan of Tony's Chocaloney explained to me why he leans into the difficulties:

> I think being overwhelmed and sometimes not sleeping is good. Making this change, it is emotional, it frustrates. Most companies are run by Excel and not by the heart. But if you want to make a business that you can be proud of, and that consumers really like, you have to include the decisions from the heart, or even make the decisions from the heart that are more important than the Excel decisions. So, the frustration bit is really good, and there is so much energy in frustration. And if you have the feeling of, 'Fuck, this needs to change,' and really deep inside have that feeling, then you are more motivated than anybody else to do things differently.

Please remember, you are needed, whole and happy.

EXERCISE Solutions starters

This solutions starter is easy – stop.

Seriously, I mean it. Put this book down, sit back, take a few deep breaths (the first might be a bit spluttery if you've

---

been shallow breathing), and consciously drop your shoulders.

If you've got time to read my brilliant book then you have time to rest your brilliant self.

Take 5 or 10 minutes before you come back for the next chapter (which is an intense one).

See you in a few.

CHAPTER ELEVEN

Signal boost

Are you called John? Statistically, that's the most likely name of someone reading this book. It's a business book after all, and there are more people called John running large corporates than there are women doing so (in the UK and the United States at least). That uncomfortable little fact played at the back of my brain while writing.

The Solutionists I know, and many whom I've interviewed and quoted in this book, are from different cultures, genders, races and perspectives. Those voices have been woven through every chapter because aspirational Solutionists come from every background. Solutionists are literally everywhere, of course they are. The great challenges of this century are truly global, so people of vision and inventiveness are working towards solutions in every community on the planet.

However, I believe that including diverse voices and hoping people get the point isn't good enough. Because, let's be realistic, many of those reading this particular book are likely to be businesspeople, with all of the aforementioned likely demographics for that readership.

Feeling uncomfortable about the way this chapter is going? Good. Being a successful Solutionist means stepping up to conversations that challenge you, with an openness to learn. It's ok to be unsure, have your preconceptions shaken and even change your mind about a few things... or many things. If you bought this book, first, thank you, and also, that means you have more discretionary income to spare than about 90 per cent of people in the world. That's a lot of privilege which can be wielded for good.

If you've been working in sustainability for some time, you know we are a big tent constantly working to improve. If you're starting a journey to becoming a Solutionist, there's a few things you need to know.

This chapter is a signal boost for the communities, voices and Solutionists historically under-valued or ignored, for the exciting answers that are emerging across the world, for the solutions needed in today's context. For a future that's already here.

To be perfectly clear, I'm a white, British, cis-gender woman writing from a perspective limited by my own experiences and biases. I know that I haven't even begun to scratch the surface of the truly global and intersectional community of Solutionists – solely because of my own limitations, notably, that I only speak English.

I don't get to claim any high ground here. However, I refuse to write a book that doesn't spread the boundaries of Solutionist relationships and acknowledge the limitations of any solution that isn't rooted in justice.

Don't worry, I think John is a very nice name.

Indigenous and traditional answers

If you're not from an indigenous community, then search out indigenous people to listen to, rather than me. I recommend reading (for starters):

- *Braiding Sweetgrass* by Robin Wall Kimmerer, a member Citizen Potawatomi Nation and Doctor of Botany. This bestseller laces together ancient indigenous knowledge with Western science – with an extraordinary set of solutions for how we heal nature, and our relationship with it.
- *Sand Talk* by Tyson Yunkaporta has the subtitle of 'How indigenous thinking can save the world'. Reminiscent of Yuval Noah Harari's *Sapiens* in its bold originality, this book plays with shapes and stories to create a coherent world view, using 'sand talk', the Aboriginal custom of drawing images on the ground to convey knowledge.
- *Fresh Banana Leaves* by Jessica Hernandez, a Maya Ch'ortí and Binnizá-Zapotec environmental scientist, reflects on the need to incorporate indigenous knowledge into how conservation works. She proposes a vision of land stewardship that heals rather than displaces, that generates rather than destroys.

Read these and you'll start a journey to appreciate the gifts that indigenous experience, and mindsets, have to offer those without that heritage.

If I'm your first introduction to a source of wisdom, solutions and thinking that too many have overlooked, I'll try my best to explain why you should listen.

While indigenous peoples comprise only 5 per cent of the human population, they safeguard 80 per cent of our remaining biodiversity (Sobrevila, 2008). That's not an accidental situation: biodiversity still exists because of indigenous experience and knowledge of how to preserve it. Today, so many of us are wracking our brains about how to align quality of life with a functioning biosphere. There are giant conferences, millions of articles and even university departments being endowed to research how to find that balance. Or, we could ask the people already doing it.

From agricultural practices that have maintained soil health and low pest damage for generations, to knowing the mix of native flora and fauna required for 'self-sustaining' habitats, to rebuilding fishing methods that are proven sustainable and revealing the medical potential of plants – the intellectual property and wise process of traditional communities is precious. It's also under threat from discrimination, exploitation and appropriation.

Uyunkar Domingo Peas Nampichkai, an indigenous Achuar leader from the Ecuadorian Amazon, told me: 'From my point of view there has to be a commitment between indigenous peoples, non-indigenous peoples, businesses, and governments to act together to save the planet. Nature is having a crisis; we all need to protect our Mother Earth. Businesses have done damage for a long time; it is time for them to start cleaning up their mess and start investing in restoration.'

Whether you're motivated by the moral cost, or potential value lost, indigenous and traditional culture is an investment necessity.

EXERCISE   Solutions starters

(There are too many diverse topics in this chapter for just one solutions starters box! So, I'm adding them after each section.)

While indigenous populations are the original Solutionists, they constitute 19 per cent of the world's poorest people (Dhir et al, 2020). Considering the vast wealth of knowledge and services they provide, this isn't a sustainable situation. Here are a few (of many more you can find) ways to start:

- Audit how your solutions/business/project already intersects with indigenous communities. Do you have operations or suppliers on traditionally owned land? Do you have indigenous colleagues, suppliers, investors? Then ask yourself, are you happy with what you found?

- Build business with indigenous communities and indigenous-owned firms – as joint venture partners and/ or suppliers. First, ask yourself – what value are you bringing to the table?

- Do your own research, just as we all should for any cultural interaction that we're not familiar with. Don't expect indigenous communities to coach or teach you how to work with them.

There are many more possible actions. However, in my experience, most non-indigenous Solutionists are either already more knowledgeable on this subject than I am, or even the few simple steps above will be entirely new and a lot of work.

Older and younger Solutionists

As Greta Thunberg said to a room full of world leaders in 2019, 'you have stolen my dreams and my childhood with your empty words... How dare you continue to look away and come here saying that you're doing enough, when the politics and solutions needed are still nowhere in sight.' Millions in her generation agree.

Born in 2003, Thunberg is a member of Gen Z – made up of people born between 1997 and 2012. Of the issues plaguing the planet and society, they list climate change and protecting the environment as their number one concern. More than half donate to charity, and 49 per cent have been selective about working in line with their personal ethics (Deloitte, 2021). One in three of these young people have taken part in a public protest (Deloitte, 2021). They want ethically and environmentally sound products and services, because they want to spend their money on things that solve problems. Over a third (36%) – more than any other age group – enjoy buying products that display their social and political beliefs (5W Public Relations, 2021). Almost half (45%) of Gen Z have boycotted a business due to its stance on an issue, compared to 39 per cent of Millennials (5W Public Relations, 2021). They are already Solutionists.

Eshita Kabra-Davies witnessed the horrors of fast fashion firsthand during a trip to her motherland, India. She saw the problem and researched solutions. Finding none – only rental models that buy stock to rent out, rely on warehouse space and require environmentally harmful dry-cleaning services – she did what any young Solutionist does – she created it. Despite having no background or experience in fashion, she launched By Rotation – the only 100 per cent peer-to-peer fashion rental platform in the UK. 'As children, we are all taught about the importance of sharing,' she says, 'but somewhere along the line this lesson gets lost.' Using By Rotation's app, people can rent their clothes to each other for a fee. Nice idea, right? The financials, though, were even better. Within two years of launch, revenue had hit six figures. In 2022 Kabra-Davies raised another £3 million in investment. As she puts it, 'By Rotation has become a green pin on the map of consumption, guiding consumers along a path to a healthier relationship with shopping' (Lavey, 2021). That's 200,000 consumers, and counting.

When seven-year-old Alina Morse was offered a lollipop by a bank teller, she wanted to say yes – but didn't want to damage her teeth. So, as the story goes, she asked her dad, 'why can't we make a lollipop that's actually good for your teeth?' Seeing a problem, she created a solution: Zolli Candy. In 2014, her vegan, sugar-free sweets hit the shelves. By 2018, Zolli Candy was taking $6 million in annual revenue. Every year since, the business has been included on Inc's 5000 list of the nation's fastest-growing private companies.

This generation are not the future, they are the now. I hope some are reading this book and stretching their Solutionist muscles ready for the race.

If you don't have a plan for Gen Z, as customers, staff, leaders and sources of breakthrough solutions – it's time you did.

While you're doing that, don't forget their grandparents. During my interview with Yoshihiro Hasebe, the CEO of Kao, we had a fantastic conversation about the centrality of youth. Then he challenged me on the realities in Japan and Europe:

> You are in Europe and I am in Japan, and our worlds, right now, are ageing societies. For a certain period of time, there will be massive numbers of people who have reached their retirement age. And those people will be the wealthiest people, they are experienced, and they have their time on their hands. They also have a powerful network, and especially the business leaders have a power of being listened to in society. I very much want them to also become Solutionists.

This idea, of both the young and the old having more freedom to move in society, is not a new one. My dear friend Bill McKibben, one of the greatest supporters of youth activism, is now turning his attention to the over 60s – with a platform called Third Act. His generation, he argues, are the ones who experienced climate stability in their youth then saw it start to crack and wobble as they aged. They know, because they lived it, that stability is possible. From volunteering to shore-up democratic institutions to investing heavily in environmental solutions – he's calling on elder Solutionists to use their retirement for leaving a positive legacy.

I hope there are retired Solutionists reading this – you are needed. Your confidence, your networks, your energy and yes, your money, are a huge part of how we solve all this.

EXERCISE   Solutions starters

I hope both younger and older Solutionists have found inspiration in this book. You might especially enjoy the concluding chapter coming up next.

In many societies, both youth and age have the privilege of speaking truth to power. This is an important role that can be taken to push for a Solutions Economy. There are also many schemes and financial packages to support young people entering entrepreneurship. More than half of small business owners in the United States are over 50 (and 17 per cent are over 60) (United States Census Bureau, 2019). One of the best parts of being a Solutionist is you can never be too young, or old, to start.

For those in the middle, like me (Gen X), we need to draw ideas, wisdom and direction from those with the youth, or age, to think differently. How to do so?

- Invite Gen Z and elders onto your Board. Not your advisory board, but as non-executives with the power to directly influence your decisions.

- Go into business with someone from a different generation; even as a part-time partner the insight and experiences are valuable.

- Find mentors from those much younger and also those older than you. Especially for younger people that works well as 'co-mentoring', where the younger person gets valuable insights for their career progress and the older can ask questions/understand youth culture.

MAPA and Global South Solutionists

The most affected people and areas (MAPA) are already experiencing devastating climate chaos. At the time of writing this book, floods in Pakistan have left 6 million people struggling to survive, just one of the latest examples of the people most affected by climate change being the same people who have done the least to cause it.

The term MAPA usually means all places in the Global South (Africa, Latin America, Pacific Islands, and so on) that likely will struggle the most with worsening weather. These are the people and places that must be front of mind for every Solutionist.

It's also where a huge percentage of the world's most innovative Solutionists can be found. Read their stories:

- *A Bigger Picture: My fight to bring a new African voice to the climate crisis* by Vanessa Nakate. It's extremely moving (and not a little humbling) reading how this girl from Kampala became a leader on the world stage. She outlines a compelling vision for the climate movement based on resilience, sustainability and equity.
- *We Have a Dream: Meet 30 young indigenous people and people of colour protecting the planet* by Dr Mya-Rose Craig. Each of these stories drew me in, from Archana Soreng, an indigenous climate activist from Rajgangpur, India, to Naila Sebbahi, a Morocco-born social, human and environmental activist. The author, Dr Mya-Rose Craig, is a 20-year-old British-Bangladeshi ornithologist who has gathered an incredible, and very hopeful, book for the future.

- *Unbowed: A memoir* by Wangarĩ Maathai. When Wangarĩ
  Maathai died in 2011, the world lost the founder of the
  Green Belt movement, the first African woman to win the
  Nobel Peace Prize and a huge voice for change. Her auto-
  biography starts with the history of British colonialism in
  Kenya, the Mau rebellion, her childhood, Kikuyu culture,
  and the experiences which inspired the birth of the Green
  Belt movement, which has planted more than 51 million
  trees in Kenya alone.

The need for loss and damage, a term referring to repara-
tions from the rich countries that cause climate change to
the poor who suffer the consequences, is well argued by
these authors. If you're not yet familiar with, or comfortable using, terms like 'climate justice', 'environmental
colonialism' and 'loss and damage', they will help you
feel ready.

This is the 21st-century agenda and it's worth speeding
your learning, and they are all brilliant, compelling and
fascinating reads!

EXERCISE   Solutions starters

Declare a climate emergency.

Are you solving climate problems only in the Global
North, or just in the atmosphere? It's all too easy to focus
only on the environmental challenges rather than realizing
that the problems, and solutions, are interdependent with
global equity and justice.

Earlier in my career, many of us in the EU and the United
States had separate 'people' and 'planet' tracks in our

strategies. I didn't feel qualified to include issues of justice and poverty in my solutions, or maybe I was just naïve. In this century, there are ample sources of help, advice and provocation to get MAPA, loss and damage, and climate justice into your plans.

All businesses' supply chains include the Global South at some degree of separation. How are you building resilience, and helping communities to adapt, so that your suppliers can overcome volatility?

Black, brown, female, neurodiverse, LGBTQIA+, disabled and other traditionally under-represented Solutionists

This is a big tent, for which the term 'intersectional' is needed. Intersectionality means that everyone has different experiences of discrimination and oppression, and we must consider everything and anything that can marginalize people – gender, race, class, sexual orientation, physical ability and so on.

Across the world, there are female Solutionists denied the right to vote and LGBTQIA+ Solutionists whose identity is illegal. Black and brown Solutionists are statistically less likely to receive funding for their answer. Disabled Solutionists are unable to access the conferences about their own solution. And there are many Solutionists for whom these barriers are multiplied by their multiple identities.

The situation is infuriating, unfair and, quite simply, stupid. We don't have time for unequal access to funding, platforms and influence – we need the best solutions for the most people and we need them now. Whenever you are presented with a suite of solutions that aren't championed by an intersectional group of Solutionists, you can be sure they aren't the best answers.

Some of the most rage-inducing and joy-triggering reads on intersectional solutions include:

- *The Intersectional Environmentalist: How to dismantle systems of oppression to protect the people + planet*, by Leah Thomas. This book is a beautiful call-to-action for us to work towards the empowerment of all people and the betterment of the planet. Leah examines the inextricable link between environmentalism, racism and privilege, and reveals the fundamental truth that we cannot save the planet without uplifting the voices of its people – especially those most often unheard.
- *Consumed: The need for collective change; colonialism, climate and consumerism* by Aja Barber. If you wear clothes you need to read this book. The first half reveals how the fashion industry mirrors colonialism by upholding global inequality. Through practical steps in the second half, we're all invited to reflect on our consumer habits and the culture of overconsumption.
- *All We Can Save*, edited by Ayana Elizabeth Johnson and Katharine K Wilkinson, includes wonderful essays (and poetry) from women, black and indigenous experts and creators. Each essay is worth reading alone, and combined they take you on a thrilling journey of truth, courage and solutions.

· In each section I've managed to confine myself to recommending only three books. For intersectional solutions an extra honourable mention must go to *Climate Justice: A man-made problem with a feminist solution* by Mary Robinson – the chair of the Elders and former UN High Commissioner for Human Rights, who pulls no punches.

As someone who has experienced the 'everyday sexism' aspect of intersectional barriers to climate action, I'm aghast at the grace with which those who experience so much more handle rampant discrimination in the climate movement. I also appreciate that anything less than grace would further the hate, trolling and exclusion they face.

EXERCISE Solutions starters

Historically excluded from leadership because of your identity? That is wrong, and your solutions are needed:

· Hold any traditional privileges? For example, white, educated, male, cis-gender, able bodied and so on. Refuse any speaker platform, roundtable, debate or pitch which doesn't represent the diversity you expect to see in the world.

· Review the diversity of your suppliers, partners, customers, investors, staff and board. Find a great diversity, equity and inclusion (DE&I) adviser, human-rights-in-supply-chain expert and inclusive leadership coach to help you correct.

- Anti-racism means fighting the biases in yourself, as well as in society. After reading these books, phrases like 'I don't see race' or 'we're a meritocracy' won't feel as comfortable as they did before. And you'll have better tools to dismantle the discrimination that's hard to acknowledge.

Answers everywhere

If you think this chapter is a bit woke, politically correct or 'right on' then you really need to read some of these books. They'll open your eyes both to the injustice and to sources of bold solutions that you might be missing.

Feel like this agenda is all too much, and the world is changing faster than you're comfortable with? I'm compassionate in response to that. I get it – loss of privilege and being de-centred in a movement can be painful, but please remember it's not as painful as exclusion or discrimination.

There is a moral necessity, and solutions opportunity, to intersectional answers that must be valued.

I also expect some readers may object to this 'separate' chapter on anti-racism and intersectional solutions. For explanation, I felt weaving intersectionality through this book still wasn't going to shine enough light on the desperate need for change.

Plus, I had a lot of great books to recommend.

Conclusion

You have the vision, grit, flex, fun and soul to make a difference. If anyone has ever told you differently, well, they were wrong. The very fact that you've dedicated your time to reading this book is proof positive that you're ready.

Reflect on your Solutionist star. This book has given you a host of tactics, which over the coming days, weeks and even years, you can use to pump your own star to burning brightness.

Do it now

We're in a perilous moment between disaster and opportunity, and everything Solutionists do right now matters. To quote our dear Intergovernmental Panel on Climate

Change one last time: 'In the scenarios we assessed, limiting warming to around 1.5°C requires global greenhouse gas emissions to peak before 2025 at the latest, and be reduced by 43% by 2030' (IPCC, 2022). They set out all the steps which would get us there, and although ambitious, none of them are impossible. The only deciding factor will be if we act, now. Millions of Solutionists already are, across the world, pushing at tipping points which can exponentially draw down emissions and raise up social justice.

One thing I heard over and again in my interviews was the futility of delaying. Like this story from Henk Jan, the CEO of Tony's Chocalonely:

> Well, I took a very slow start. So, my parents were not educated, I was the first to go to university. I started working at Heineken, then Innocent Drinks, and then Tony's. I thought I have to suck in all the lessons available, learn a lot, because who am I, what do I know? In hindsight, it took me too long before I was an entrepreneur. And to be completely honest, I could have had more confidence in the beginning of becoming an entrepreneur. So, some people that I meet are 20 years younger and are in business as long as I am! I could have sped up if I'd had little bit of the Nike feeling of 'Just do it'. That's one of the lessons I've now learnt: to always take decisions proactively. So, I don't wait.

I hope I've conveyed the rewards of becoming a Solutionist, both financial and emotional. Those prizes are available right now and will only grow as we speed towards the Solutions Economy. I was also very moved by another incentive for urgency that Paul Polman presented to me – the moral imperative: 'If you won this lottery ticket of life, with an education, medical care, food, access to electricity and toilet, well, you're in only 5 per cent of the world's population, and you need to put yourself to the service of the other 95 per cent. So, I stay hopeful, because I know any other path, and it might be stupid, but any other path doesn't lead to anything. And we frankly don't have a choice. I sometimes say, and people laugh, but I sometimes say, "It's too late to be a pessimist".'

Personally, I'm happy if you're a Solutionist in order to make your fortune, become famous or prove to your high-school bully that you can change the world. However, I know that most of the people reading this book will resonate with Paul's words. While being a Solutionist is fun and financially rewarding, that's not why most of us chose this path. We're Solutionists because we can't not be.

If the IPCC maths is right, we have eight years to save the world.

Choose your adventure

All this urgency might feel thrilling, and perhaps you've sketched out some plans based on the exercises I've set. Or you might already be deep into your solutions journey and have used this book to hone your skills and gird yourself for the next giant step. Or… you're still wondering what to do with your star.

The problems are complex; there are big problems, with multiple branching-off problems, leading to tiny but intractable problem-ets – it's a permacrisis. Sometimes it can feel like you've been asked to fight against human nature itself or unpick centuries of structures that are resistant to change.

The best way to decide what to do is to ask yourself, what would I most enjoy? Not what would make the most difference, not what the world wants, not what you think 'needs' doing. Instead, what would bring you the most personal joy to work on every day.

What many people don't realize is that the 'fun' point of the star is where to start in finding your solution.

Grab a slip of paper and quickly brainstorm everything you could do that would make a difference. For example:

- Pitch to my boss that breakthrough solutions idea I had.
- Start a side hustle of that eco-business idea I've been thinking about.
- Sign up for an online course about sustainability.
- Start a 'Solutionist team' at work, for those passionate about change.
- Finish that book/blog post I've been working on.
- Build a business case for our company to pivot into solutions.
- Look for promising solutions start-ups to invest in.
- Sketch out a list of who might help me with my idea.
- Register for some online events/talks about sustainability.
- Offer to be a non-executive/trustee of solutions start-ups.
- Create a presentation about solutions to inspire my team.
- Find online communities of Solutionists for support.

Then, looking at your list, think about what would be most fulfilling, most fun, most personally exciting. Force yourself to be intensely selfish. If there's nothing on the list that shoots a little thrill up your spine – then it's the wrong list. You must be truly, madly, deeply motivated by the solutions you're going to dedicate yourself to.

As CEO of Futerra, Lucy Shea, always tells me, 'make it fun if you want it done'.

A sense of duty, responsibility and martyr-like commitment will only ever get you so far. People don't burn out doing what they love, but they burn out all the time doing what they 'should' do.

You might be nodding along while still thinking, 'Ok, but actually, I need to do what will make the biggest difference, irrespective of my own personal feelings about it'.

Please don't. We need your happiness as much as your hard work. Every Solutionist I spoke to, even those who were having bad days, absolutely love what they do. Not one was sacrificing anything to do it, because they all draw a deep sense of personal fulfilment from the solutions they've chosen to work on. Having fun is what makes them successful.

Find Solutionists

A community of Solutionists will always be more successful than a lone changemaker. When I asked Yoshihiro Hasebe of Kao what advice he would give to other CEOs seeking to implement transformative sustainability plans, he answered:

> I believe that 50% of effort should go to your own company but the other 50% should go over the wall of your company, and make team players out of the other companies, so that

you can work together. If business leaders can practise that with their own technologies and the resources, and by working with others, they will find so many things that they can achieve at a high level. But, in order to do that, you have to have an open, wide heart, and you need courage. This is my message, and please tell the other leaders you interview, 'Have a big heart and be courageous.'

This was a message I heard from so many of these success-ful, competitive, growing businesses.

Aron Cramer, CEO of Business For Social Responsibility, who represents over 300 leading companies, implores us to:

Get out of the bubble! Learn how to persuade people who are neutral or opposed to sustainability. We live in a bubble and are too convinced that we have 'the truth'. Conveying 'the truth' deepens the commitment from people who already agree. It is a turn-off for those who don't. Real progress comes when we show – not tell – what a better world looks like.

Vaitea from Enapter is probably the youngest entrepreneur I interviewed. She had such wisdom on what it takes to lead with this openness:

I have been questioning what kind of leader do I want to be. I think I'm more and more coming to peace with a vulnerable leadership style, because in the past I was not. I really do want to lead with vulnerability. In this movement, for sure, you need strength and you need resilience and you need to fight, right? But, I also think that leading with vulnerability can also create the softness and the type of connection and foundation that you need to connect with

your colleagues and others on a level that is going to make
things happen. So, I'm doing vulnerability, and not everyone
is open to it, but this is how I'm going to lead.

Because we're all working at the edge of what is possible,
rather than treading well-worn paths, I think this vulnerability that Vaitea and Hasbe-san speak of is vital. When
you're the first to do something, it's obvious you'll have
to say at some point, 'I don't know the answer to that'.
Familiarize yourself with how the words, 'I don't know',
'I got that wrong' and 'It might not work' feel as you say
them. I've discovered there is a wonderful power to that
openness; it draws people in and warms a room.

In this book I've only had space to profile very few of
the wonderful Solutionists that I know. In this limited
sample, I hope you've experienced at least a taste or echo
of the warmth, humour, humility and simple friendliness
I felt from every one of them. And which I feel every day
working in the Solutionist community.

I hope you feel empowered to join it.

You, yes you

As we come to the closing of this book, I have one final
secret of Solutionist success to share with you. It's not a
tactic, tool or strategy. Not a point on the star. It's not even
a wonderful IPCC fact or Solutionist case study. Yet,
perhaps, it might be the most important thing to remember
on your Solutionist journey: Confidence isn't an emotion,
it's a skill.

Very few people, including the amazing people in this book, often feel confident. This is one of those secrets of life that some people learn early and others too late. So many Solutionists-in-waiting expect to wake up one morning with the confidence to make the changes they've been thinking about. Or they watch confidence-guru videos and find mentors to help boost them up – chasing that feeling of finally 'being confident enough' to do the thing.

Sorry, never going to happen. You will never feel confident enough. You're going to have to do it anyway.

You can learn the skills of confidence – good writing skills, strong presentation skills, skilled decision making, skilled negotiation and so on. You can become knowledgeable in your solution and experienced in your subject. And that's it – you will be skilled and knowledgeable – and that's all that is possible. There isn't a secret sauce of confidence which suddenly means you can do things without feeling scared. The secret is that there is no sauce.

The thing which holds back so many potential Solutionists is waiting for permission. In my interviews I heard wonderful stories of Solutionists who experienced that unlocking. Like Kate Brandt's experience at the US Navy:

> Ray Mabus was Secretary of the Navy and I was his energy adviser. And I really admire that, when I was very early in my career, he gave me a huge amount of responsibility. He really invited me to be his strategist and partner in thinking about how we could take the Department of the Navy, which is one of the world's largest energy users, and change how it's powered. So, I'm very grateful to him and happily still really close with him and still get the benefits of his insights and wisdom.

Or Majora Carter's moment of permission:

> Early on, I went to work in service of an amazing community activist because I thought she was brilliant, and I just wanted to help her do what she did. At one point, she turned at me and was just like, 'Why aren't you doing this? Why are you researching speeches so I can say it, why don't you say it? Why aren't you the one out there talking to people?' And I was just like, 'Well, because that's just not what I do,' and she just said, 'You have every right to speak on behalf of your people,' and I was just like, 'Oh.' It was a difficult moment, because I didn't want to do it, because I had an image of me which is, 'I don't talk in public, I don't need to, I'm perfectly fine,' I just didn't feel like I could do things like that. If Yolanda hadn't been pushing me, I don't know if I'd be where I am right now, I really don't, because that was one of the first times anybody said to me, 'Why not you?'

Everyone has imposter syndrome and sustainability makes that even worse – who are we to be trying to change the world? Real confidence is about feeling neurotic and inadequate and doing it anyway. Which is excellent news. Because it means you're ready. You don't have to wait for that mythical confident feeling to finally drape across your shoulders and make you worthy. You, and every other Solutionist, are going to muddle through, making embarrassing mistakes, tripping up, falling flat and yet doing it anyway. Because that's all that anyone ever does.

Not everyone has someone as wonderful and wise as Ray or Yolanda in their life to kick through the myth of confidence and say, 'Why not you?'

So, I'll do it. Why not you?

You are a Solutionist. Now, go save the damn planet.

References

Introduction

Brown, J (2019) How Tony's Chocolonely chocolate brand plans to end slavery, *The Independent*, 10 May

Nelson, J (2019) Chapter 4: No smallholder farmer left behind, in *Leave No One Behind: Time for specifics on the sustainable development goals, eds* H Kharas, J W McArthur and I Ohno, p 60, Brookings Institution Press, Washington, DC

NORC (2020) Final Report: Assessing Progress in Reducing Child Labor in Cocoa Production in Côte d'Ivoire and Ghana, NORC at the University of Chicago. www.norc.org/Research/Projects/Pages/assessing-progress-in-reducing-child-labor-in-cocoa-growing-areas-of-c%C3%B4te-d%E2%80%99ivoire-and-ghana.aspx (archived at https://perma.cc/R7Q6-NDKS)

Walk Free Foundation (2018) The Global Slavery Index, 2018. https://downloads.globalslaveryindex.org/ephemeral/GSI-2018_FNL_190828_CO_DIGITAL_P-1667391852.pdf (archived at https://perma.cc/V9GS-WR8P)

Chapter 1: Welcome to the Solutionist Economy

Clifton, J (2017) The world's broken workplace, *Gallup*, June 13

Google (2022) Accelerating climate action at Google and beyond: A progress update, p 26. www.gstatic.com/gumdrop/sustainability/google-2022-climate-action-progress-update.pdf (archived at https://perma.cc/MT72-J8EM)

Graeber, D (2018) *Bullshit Jobs: A theory*, Allen Lane, London

Hansard (1806) HC Slave Importation Bill, 1 May, vol 6 cc1021–5

IMF (2022) Fossil fuel subsidies. www.imf.org/en/Topics/climate-change/energy-subsidies (archived at https://perma.cc/44LN-ZV26)

International Cooperative Alliance (2016) Facts and figures. www.ica.coop/en/cooperatives/facts-and-figures (archived at https://perma.cc/PJ37-ZQRL)

Mazzucato, M (2019) What is economic value, and who creates it? TED talk (online video). www.ted.com/talks/mariana_mazzucato_what_is_economic_value_and_who_creates_it/ (archived at https://perma.cc/Q3XQ-Z8RK)

McKinsey & Co (2022) Playing offense to create value in the net-zero transition, April 13. www.mckinsey.com/capabilities/sustainability/our-insights/playing-offense-to-create-value-in-the-net-zero-transition (archived at https://perma.cc/PN2N-43SK)

Meyer, R (2022) The climate economy is about to explode, *The Atlantic*, 5 October. www.theatlantic.com/science/archive/2022/10/inflation-reduction-act-climate-economy/671659/ (archived at https://perma.cc/62AE-4V2D)

SBTi (2021) SBTi launches world-first net-zero corporate standard, 28 October. https://sciencebasedtargets.org/news/sbti-launches-world-first-net-zero-corporate-standard (archived at https://perma.cc/XLW7-3Q35)

Statista (2022) Number of visits to IKEA stores worldwide from 2010 to 2021. www.statista.com/statistics/241828/number-of-visits-to-ikea-stores-worldwide/ (archived at https://perma.cc/9KW6-SF9K)

The World Counts (2022) Global waste problem. www.theworldcounts.com/challenges/waste/global-waste-problem (archived at https://perma.cc/94NJ-AC94)

UNDP in Asia and the Pacific (2021) Frankie the dinosaur has a message for humanity (online video). www.youtube.com/watch?v=L9eFABJqGTM (archived at https://perma.cc/WM5N-WUT6)

UNEP (2021) Addendum to the Emissions Gap Report 2021, https://wedocs.unep.org/20.500.11822/37350 (archived at https://perma.cc/QWN7-RTQE)

US Congress (2022) Summary: The Inflation Reduction Act 2022, www.congress.gov/bill/117th-congress/house-bill/5376/text (archived at https://perma.cc/B5HE-NEEV)

Wittenberg-Cox, A (2020) 5 economists redefining everything: Oh yes, and they're women, *Forbes*, 31 May 2020. www.forbes.com/ sites/avivahwittenbergcox/2020/05/31/5-economists-redefining-everything--oh-yes-and-theyre-women/?sh=729dfd2a714a (archived at https://perma.cc/8D9S-WHXQ)

World Bank (2021) Population, Total. https://data.worldbank.org/ indicator/SP.POP.TOTL (archived at https://perma.cc/R6VU-E5T9)

World Bank (2022) Fact sheet: an adjustment to global poverty lines. www.worldbank.org/en/news/factsheet/2022/05/02/ fact-sheet-an-adjustment-to-global-poverty-lines (archived at https://perma.cc/XB56-4EKG)

Chapter 2: Your star

Anderson, R C (2007) Interview with Dean, C. Ray Anderson: Executive on a mission: Saving the planet, *New York Times*, 22 May

Carson, R (1963) *Silent Spring*, Houghton Mifflin, Boston, MA

Enapter (2021) Enapter named as Earthshot Prize finalist [blog], enapter.com, 17 September. www.enapter.com/newsroom/ earthshot-prize (archived at https://perma.cc/V34C-AAQ8)

Kennedy, R F (1966) Day of Affirmation Address. www.jfklibrary. org/learn/about-jfk/the-kennedy-family/robert-f-kennedy/ robert-f-kennedy-speeches/day-of-affirmation-address-university-of-capetown-capetown-south-africa-june-6-1966 (archived at https://perma.cc/LY8C-T8V6)

Maathai, W in Sears, P (1991) You Strike the Woman…, *In Context*, vol 28, 'Making it Happen', Spring, Context Institute, Bainbridge Island, Washington, WA

Chapter 4: The Mississippi mind

Dweck, C S (2014) The power of yet, TED talk (online video). www.ted.com/talks/carol_dweck_the_power_of_believing_that_ you_can_improve/transcript?language=en (archived at https:// perma.cc/4D3R-S2F6)

Chapter 5: Fix it formula

IPCC (2022) Climate Change 2022: Mitigation of climate change – Working Group III contribution to the Sixth Assessment Report of the Intergovernmental Panel on Climate Change. www.ipcc. ch/report/ar6/wg3/ (archived at https://perma.cc/EVY9-KXXR)

Chapter 6: Hope is a business plan

Adams, R (2019) Cycle Superhighways in Denmark's Capital Region. https://handshakecycling.eu/news/cycle-superhighways-denmark%E2%80%99s-capital-region (archived at https:// perma.cc/BQ5P-5MN6)

Benton, T G et al (2021) Food system impacts on biodiversity loss: Three levers for food system transformation in support of nature, p 7, Chatham House, London

BIS (2020) CT2: Banknotes and coins in circulation. https://stats. bis.org/statx/srs/table/CT2?m=1 (archived at https://perma. cc/4L6F-DSP4)

BITC (2020) Factsheet: Living sustainably in lockdown, p 1, BITC, London

Brock, A and Williams, I (2020) Ranked: The environmental impact of five different soft drink containers. https://theconversation.com/ranked-the-environmental-impact-of-five-different-soft-drink-containers-149642 (archived at https://perma.cc/63RJ-RRL6)

Business Norway (2018) Small sensors solve big problems. www.theexplorer.no/solutions/Neuron-Sensors-Small-sensors-solve-big-problems/ (archived at https://perma.cc/4QQY-B8W7)

C40 (2018) Summary for urban policymakers: What the IPCC Special Report on Global Warming of 1.5°C means for cities, p 16, Brussels, Global Covenant of Mayors for Climate & Energy

CEIC (2022) Money supply M1 & M2. www.ceicdata.com/en/indicators (archived at https://perma.cc/Z5AQ-9Z5C)

Climate Investigations Center (2019) Energy and corporate trade associations spend $1.4 billion on PR campaigns. https://climateinvestigations.org/energy-trade-associations-spend-pr/ (archived at https://perma.cc/FP57-L4YG)

Coalition for Urban Transitions (2019) The new urban opportunity, p 69, Coalition for Urban Transitions

Coursera (2021) Impact report. https://about.coursera.org/press/wp-content/uploads/2021/11/2021-Coursera-Impact-Report.pdf (archived at https://perma.cc/G9W9-ATS9)

Creatore, M I et al (2016) Association of neighborhood walkability with change in overweight, obesity, and diabetes, *Journal of the American Medical Association*, 315 (20), p 2211. doi: 10.1001/jama.2016.5898 (archived at https://perma.cc/59XM-Q4KX)

De Vos, J M et al (2014) Estimating the normal background rate of species extinction, *Conservation Biology*, 29 (2), pp 452–62. doi: 10.1111/cobi.12380 (archived at https://perma.cc/M8X2-5GET)

Demirguc-Kunt, A et al (2021) The Global Findex Database 2021, Worldbank.org. doi: 10.1596/978-1-4648-1897-4 (archived at https://perma.cc/5VXT-MZKY)

DL1961 (2022) Sustainable materials. www.dl1961.com/pages/
sustainable-materials (archived at https://perma.cc/DG6W-
7YGT)

Ericsson (2017) 5G by Ericsson. www.ericsson.com/en/5g (archived
at https://perma.cc/5AFR-GJPW)

Ethereum (2022) Ethereum energy consumption. https://ethereum.
org/en/energy-consumption/#fn-1 (archived at https://perma.cc/
GY86-3QCK)

Exponential Roadmap (2019) Scaling 36 solutions to halve
emissions by 2030. https://exponentialroadmap.org/wp-content/
uploads/2019/09/Exponential-Roadmap-1.5-September-19-2019.
pdf (archived at https://perma.cc/5C9Q-QUCP)

EY (2015) Cultural times: The first global map of cultural and
creative industries, p 8, EY

FAO (2022a) FRA 2020 Remote Sensing Survey, Rome, IT: FAO,
p 47. doi: 10.4060/cb9970en (archived at https://perma.cc/7DJL-
JFC3)

FAO (2022b) Get involved – international day of awareness of
food loss and waste, p 3, FAO

Financial Times (2007) FT Global 500, December. http://media.
ft.com/cms/813c979e-0faa-11dd-8871-0000779fd2ac (archived
at https://perma.cc/9S23-Y7TC)

Financial Times (2017) FT Global

Friends of the Earth EU (2021) Meat Atlas 2021, p 12, Friends of
the Earth EU, London

GABC (2021) 2021 Global status report for buildings and
construction, p 12, Global Alliance for Buildings and Construction

Gartner (2019) Hype cycle for smart city technologies and
solutions, Gartner

Google (2022) Accelerating climate action at Google and beyond:
A progress update. www.gstatic.com/gumdrop/sustainability/
google-2022-climate-action-progress-update.pdf (archived at
https://perma.cc/G7LX-49Q8)

Gustavsson, J et al (2011) Global food losses and food waste, p 4, FAO, Rome, IT

GVR (2020) Energy retrofit systems market size, share & trends analysis report by application (residential, non-residential), by product (LED retrofit lighting, envelope), by region (Europe, APAC), and segment forecasts, 2020–2028, Grand View Research

GWI (2017) The demographics of Uber's US users, Global Web Index. https://blog.gwi.com/chart-of-the-day/uber-demographics/ (archived at https://perma.cc/HS94-5RWM)

Hampson, L (2022) Veganuary having 'biggest year ever' with over 600,000 sign-ups. www.independent.co.uk/life-style/food-and-drink/veganuary-2022-vegan-people-health-b1995557.html (archived at https://perma.cc/8TJ5-MWU2)

IEA (2022) World energy investment 2022, p 32, International Energy Agency

Imperial College London (2020) Drones that patrol forests could monitor environmental and ecological changes, *ScienceDaily*, 3 November. www.sciencedaily.com/releases/2020/11/201103112526.htm (archived at https://perma.cc/U96K-VWPN)

IPCC (2022) Climate Change 2022: Mitigation of climate change - Working Group III contribution to the Sixth Assessment Report of the Intergovernmental Panel on Climate Change. www.ipcc.ch/report/ar6/wg3/ (archived at https://perma.cc/EVY9-KXXR)

IRENA (2017) Renewable power: Sharply falling generation costs, p 2, International Renewable Energy Agency

IRENA (2019) Renewable energy now accounts for a third of global power capacity. www.irena.org/news/pressreleases/2019/Apr/renewable-energy-now-accounts-for-a-third-of-global-power-capacity (archived at https://perma.cc/5NV2-EJ7M)

Jambeck, J R et al (2015) Plastic waste inputs from land into the ocean, *Science*, 347 (6223), pp 768–71. doi: 10.1126/science.1260352 (archived at https://perma.cc/VQ5V-H3ZK)

Kommenda, N (2019) How your flight emits as much CO_2 as many people do in a year. www.theguardian.com/environment/

ng-interactive/2019/jul/19/carbon-calculator-how-taking-one-flight-emits-as-much-as-many-people-do-in-a-year (archived at https://perma.cc/3LGD-6DLU)

Lee, J (2008) Big tobacco's spin on women's liberation, *The New York Times*, 10 October

Lorente, J G (2016) The creative economy: The new El Dorado that Europe and Latin America want to lead, IE Insights. www.ie.edu/insights/articles/the-creative-economy-the-new-dorado-that-europe-and-latin-america-want-to-lead/ (archived at https://perma.cc/3BT9-KSUW)

McKinsey (2021) Call for action: Seizing the decarbonization opportunity in construction, McKinsey

Mezzanine (2020) DigiFarm. https://mezzanineware.com/digital-productivity-technology/technology-solutions-for-agribusiness/digital-solution-smallholder-farmers/ (archived at https://perma.cc/94TR-AC7S)

Movin'On (2021) New generation's view on the future of mobility in a (post)-Covid world, p 4, Movin'On

NASA (2016) NASA, Scripps Institution of Oceanography shake-up earthquake warning systems. www.nasa.gov/feature/goddard/2016/nasa-scripps-institution-of-oceanography-shake-up-earthquake-warning-systems (archived at https://perma.cc/6KAE-EYYH)

Neate, R (2021) Airships for city hops could cut flying's CO_2 emissions by 90%. www.theguardian.com/world/2021/may/26/airships-for-city-hops-could-cut-flyings-co2-emissions-by-90 (archived at https://perma.cc/C6LX-6K6B)

Olivier, J G et al (2016) Trends in global CO_2 emissions 2016 report, pp 64–5, PBL Netherlands Environmental Assessment Agency, The Hague

Project Drawdown (2020) Walkable cities. https://drawdown.org/solutions/walkable-cities (archived at https://perma.cc/P7U3-2E96)

PYMNTS (2021) The healthcare payment experience report, p 7, PYMNTS

Reed, D (2015) How Curitiba's BRT stations sparked a transport revolution – a history of cities in 50 buildings, day 43. www.theguardian.com/cities/2015/may/26/curitiba-brazil-brt-transport-revolution-history-cities-50-buildings (archived at https://perma.cc/RU36-EPSC)

Ritchie, H (2019) Half of the world's habitable land is used for agriculture. https://ourworldindata.org/global-land-for-agriculture (archived at https://perma.cc/SV5D-4DEF)

Ritchie, H (2020) Climate change and flying: What share of global CO_2 emissions come from aviation? https://ourworldindata.org/co2-emissions-from-aviation (archived at https://perma.cc/3EPY-8U2T)

Ritchie, H, Roser, M and Rosado, P (2020) CO_2 and GHG emissions by sector. https://ourworldindata.org/emissions-by-sector#energy-electricity-heat-and-transport-73-2 (archived at https://perma.cc/E68G-SRQV)

Scarr, S (2019) A plateful of plastic. https://graphics.reuters.com/ENVIRONMENT-PLASTIC/0100B4TF2MQ/index.html (archived at https://perma.cc/U2TD-BS36)

Sivak, M and Schoettle, B (2016) Recent decreases in the proportion of persons with a driver's license across all age groups, p 2, The University of Michigan

Sobrevila, C (2008) The role of indigenous peoples in biodiversity conservation, p xii, World Bank Group, Washington, DC. documents.worldbank.org (archived at https://perma.cc/V7Y3-WHKB)

The Fabricant (2020) Iridescence. www.thefabricant.com/iridescence (archived at https://perma.cc/PRE9-P7LT)

The Royal Society (2020) Digital technology and the planet: Harnessing computing to achieve net zero. https://royalsociety.org/-/media/policy/projects/digital-technology-and-the-planet/digital-technology-and-the-planet-report.pdf (archived at https://perma.cc/PE3N-ADQ2)

The World Counts (2020) The world counts. www.theworldcounts. com/challenges/planet-earth/mining/environmental-impact-of-steel-production (archived at https://perma.cc/4JAP-TBPG)

Thinking Ahead Institute (2022) Global pension assets study | 2022, p 6, Thinking Ahead Institute, London

Thomas, O Z and Dillard, R (2022) A new way of making dairy: Perceptions, naming and implications. https://formo. bio/a-new-way (archived at https://perma.cc/8K2U-X7QZ)

TIME (1950) The press: Mimosa, moonbeams and memory, 30 January. https://content.time.com/time/subscriber/ article/0,33009,856518,00.html (archived at https://perma.cc/ UHB5-YDJW)

Townsend, S (2021) Are ad agencies, PR firms and lobbyists destroying the climate? TED talk (online video). www.ted.com/ talks/solitaire_townsend_are_ad_agencies_pr_firms_and_ lobbyists_destroying_the_climate?language=en (archived at https://perma.cc/7GU7-CNRA)

UNCCD (2017) The global land outlook, p 52, United Nations Convention to Combat Desertification, Bonn, DE

UNEP (2009) UNEP Year Book 2009, p 45, UNEP

UNEP (2020) No time to waste: Using data to drive down food waste. www.unep.org/news-and-stories/story/no-time-waste-using-data-drive-down-food-waste (archived at https://perma. cc/4BPD-PCFE)

UNEP (2021) Becoming #GenerationRestoration: Ecosystem restoration for people, nature and climate, p 3, UNEP

UNESCO (2017) Reshaping cultural policies: Advancing creativity for development, p 36, UNESCO, Paris

UNFCCC (2019) MAX burgers: Creating the world's first 'climate positive' menu. https://unfccc.int/climate-action/momentum-for-change/climate-neutral-now/max-burgers (archived at https:// perma.cc/DUU5-QMNA)

WGBC (2022) The commitment, World Green Building Council. https://worldgbc.org/advancing-net-zero/the-commitment/ (archived at https://perma.cc/EBJ8-TE86)

World Inequality Lab (2022) *World Inequality Report 2022*, p 10, Harvard University Press, Cambridge, MA

Wunsch, N G (2021) Vegan food market: Global market value 2025. www.statista.com/statistics/1280275/value-of-the-global-vegan-food-market/ (archived at https://perma.cc/W9C5-R96J)

WWF (2021) Driven to waste: The global impact of food loss and waste on farms, p 6, WWF UK, Surrey, UK

Xu, X et al (2021) Global greenhouse gas emissions from animal-based foods are twice those of plant-based foods, *Nature Food*, 2 (9), pp 724–32. doi: 10.1038/s43016-021-00358-x (archived at https://perma.cc/36QH-472L)

Yakowicz, W (2019) 14 months, 120 cities, \$2 billion: There's never been a company like Bird. Is the world ready? *Inc. Magazine*, February. www.inc.com/magazine/201902/will-yakowicz/bird-electric-scooter-travis-vanderzanden-2018-company-of-the-year.html (archived at https://perma.cc/FDW3-3V38)

Chapter 7: The quarter rule

Bu, C (2022) What Norway can teach the world about electric vehicles. https://time.com/6133180/norway-electric-vehicles/ (archived at https://perma.cc/PX7P-4N3Y)

Centola, D et al (2018) Experimental evidence for tipping points in social convention, *Science*, 360 (6393), pp 1116–19. doi: 10.1126/science.aas8827 (archived at https://perma.cc/PT9H-W6BN)

Chenoweth, E (2013) The success of nonviolent civil resistance, TEDx Talks (online video). www.youtube.com/watch?v=YJSehRlU34w (archived at https://perma.cc/7TTW-CT49)

Ernst & Young (2022) Tipping point reached as more than half of global car buyers seek electric vehicle for the first time. www.ey.com/en_gl/news/2022/05/tipping-point-reached-as-more-than-half-of-global-car-buyers-see-electric-vehicle-for-the-first-time (archived at https://perma.cc/CE26-UXYV)

Gladwell, M (2000) *The Tipping Point: How little things can make a big difference*, Little, Brown, Boston, MA

Good Food Institute (2022) 2021 U.S. Retail Market Insights, p 3, Good Food Institute

IPCC (2015) *Climate Change 2014: Mitigation of climate change*, Cambridge University Press, Cambridge, UK. doi: 10.1017/cbo9781107415416 (archived at https://perma.cc/XD4R-R4N5)

IPCC (2021) *Climate change 2021: The physical science basis. Contribution of Working Group I to the Sixth Assessment Report of the Intergovernmental Panel on Climate Change*, eds V Masson-Delmotteet al, Cambridge University Press, Cambridge. doi: 10.1017/9781009157896 (archived at https://perma.cc/TVR8-FLN5)

IPCC (2022) *Climate change 2022: Impacts, adaptation, and vulnerability. Contribution of Working Group II to the Sixth Assessment Report of the Intergovernmental Panel on Climate Change,* eds H-O Pörtner et al, Cambridge University Press, Cambridge. doi: 10.1017/9781009325844 (archived at https://perma.cc/TGU3-28HK)

Norsk Elbilforening (2022) A milestone for electric cars in Norway. https://elbil.no/a-milestone-for-electric-cars-in-norway/ (archived at https://perma.cc/3TXQ-KJDE)

Roberts, S (2007) 51% of women are now living without spouse, *The New York Times*, 16 January

Roof, K and Tan, G (2021) Impossible Foods eyes $7 billion valuation in fundraising, *Bloomberg*, 28 October. www.bloomberg.com/news/articles/2021-10-28/impossible-foods-is-said-to-eye-7-billion-value-in-fundraising (archived at https://perma.cc/SV6R-X6E8)

Smart Protein Project (2021) What consumers want: A survey on European consumer attitudes towards plant-based foods, p 11. https://smartproteinproject.eu/consumer-attitudes-plant-based-food-report/ (archived at https://perma.cc/W36X-FHF8)

Statista (2021) Global: Milk substitute consumption 2013–2026. www.statista.com/forecasts/1277816/milk-substitute-global-consumption (archived at https://perma.cc/J8R6-XPE7)

Tribou, A and Collins, K (2015) This is how fast America changes its mind, *Bloomberg*, 26 June. www.bloomberg.com/graphics/2015-pace-of-social-change/ (archived at https://perma.cc/A8JN-8LQP)

UN (2019) Ozone on track to heal completely in our lifetime, UN Environment Agency declares on World Day. https://news.un.org/en/story/2019/09/1046452 (archived at https://perma.cc/J279-XZT5)

Veganuary (2019) Veganuary 2019: The results are in! https://veganuary.com/veganuary-2019-the-results-are-in/ (archived at https://perma.cc/XQK4-E54G)

Veganuary (2022) About us. https://veganuary.com/about/about-us/ (archived at https://perma.cc/U6LD-CLS5)

Wunderling, N et al (2021) Interacting tipping elements increase risk of climate domino effects under global warming, *Earth System Dynamics*, 12(2), pp 601–19. doi: 10.5194/esd-12-601-2021 (archived at https://perma.cc/3WJY-KPES).

Chapter 8: Storytelling the solutions

Bruner, J (1986) *Actual Minds, Possible Worlds*, Harvard University Press, Cambridge, MA

European Commission (2021) Screening of websites for 'greenwashing': Half of green claims lack evidence. https://ec.europa.eu/commission/presscorner/detail/en/ip_21_269 (archived at https://perma.cc/BZ25-NJGA)

Freling, T H et al (2020) When poignant stories outweigh cold hard facts: A meta-analysis of the anecdotal bias, *Organizational Behaviour and Human Decision Processes*, 160 (Sept), pp 51–67

Futerra (2019) The honest generation, p 21, Futerra

Futerra and Ipsos MORI (2021) The solutions survey. https://docs.
google.com/presentation/d/1ayN3mzzEYTvUVQ7T-DHiQbrvNw
2BOUGaSp22R2gACPQ/edit#slide=id.gf86077d83b_15_0
(archived at https://perma.cc/58FZ-9AT8)

Chapter 9: Myths and traps

Chen, C (2018) How open-source innovation may transform
fashion. www.businessoffashion.com/articles/news-analysis/
how-open-source-innovation-may-transform-fashion/ (archived
at https://perma.cc/BB7L-HS9F)

Futerra and Ipsos MORI (2021) The solutions survey. https://docs.
google.com/presentation/d/1ayN3mzzEYTvUVQ7T-DHiQbrvNw
2BOUGaSp22R2gACPQ/edit#slide=id.gf86077d83b_15_0
(archived at https://perma.cc/KT29-8T32)

Kantar (2020) The Brand Bravery Benchmark, p 5, Kantar. https://
www.kantar.com/inspiration/brands/the-brand-bravery-
benchmark (archived at https://perma.cc/8XHQ-H6JE)

SWNS Media Group (2021) More than two thirds of consumers
want brands to do more to reduce waste. https://swnsdigital.
com/uk/2021/04/more-than-two-thirds-of-consumers-want-
brands-to-do-more-to-reduce-waste/ (archived at https://perma.
cc/V6NR-FEV6)

Chapter 10: Joyful entrepreneurship

Bloom, P (2019) The case against empathy, 16 January. www.vox.
com/conversations/2017/1/19/14266230/empathy-morality-
ethics-psychology-compassion-paul-bloom (archived at https://
perma.cc/C8AG-WYZU)

Indeed (2021) Introducing the Indeed work happiness score, p 4.
www.orgdch.org/wp-content/uploads/2021/06/US-Introducing-
the-Indeed-Happiness-Score.pdf (archived at https://perma.
cc/2LF8-7F4T)

Ioan, A (2021) A global study of the lives and work of young social
innovators, *The Possibilists*, p 26. https://thepossibilists.org/
wp-content/uploads/2021/06/The-Possibilists-Academic-Study-
Report.pdf (archived at https://perma.cc/7KFN-HVYQ)

Krumina, K (2017) New data proves staying late in the office is
pointless. https://observer.com/2017/11/new-data-proves-
staying-late-in-the-office-is-pointless/ (archived at https://perma.
cc/T6WT-NFGD)

McKinsey & Company (2021) What employees are saying about
the future of remote work. www.mckinsey.com/capabilities/
people-and-organizational-performance/our-insights/what-
employees-are-saying-about-the-future-of-remote-work
(archived at https://perma.cc/43AL-7KE5)

Pencavel, J H (2014) The productivity of working hours, p 21,
Institute of Labor Economics (IZA), Bonn, DE. doi: 10.2139/
ssrn.2429648 (archived at https://perma.cc/9VBF-2H7M)

Randstad (2019) Randstad Workmonitor Q4 2019, p 37. https://
workforceinsights.randstad.com/hr-research-reports-
workmonitor-q42019 (archived at https://perma.cc/AJ2F-YDLR)

Windcall Institute (2009) Impact – Windcall Institute. https://
windcall.org/about/impact/ (archived at https://perma.cc/
F6GU-FQ98)

Chapter 11: Signal boost

5W Public Relations (2021) 2021 Consumer culture report, p 9.
www.5wpr.com/new/wp-content/uploads/pdf/5WPR_
ConsumerReport_2021.pdf (archived at https://perma.cc/9F6X-
LBMV)

Deloitte (2021) The Deloitte Global 2021 Millennial and Gen Z survey, p 28. www2.deloitte.com/cn/en/pages/about-deloitte/articles/pr-millennialsurvey-2021.html (archived at https://perma.cc/RN36-432N)

Dhir, R K et al (2020) Implementing the ILO Indigenous and Tribal Peoples Convention No. 169: Towards an inclusive, sustainable and just future, p 20, International Labor Organization (ILO), Geneva, Switzerland. www.ilo.org/wcmsp5/groups/public/---dgreports/---dcomm/---publ/documents/publication/wcms_735607.pdf (archived at https://perma.cc/8YGW-N65D)

Lavey, K (2021) Founder of By Rotation: From side hustle to six-figure business. www.drapersonline.com/insight/founder-of-by-rotation-from-side-hustle-to-six-figure-business (archived at https://perma.cc/3U98-BSHM)

Sobrevila, C (2008) The role of indigenous peoples in biodiversity conservation, p xii, World Bank Group, Washington, DC. documents.worldbank.org (archived at https://perma.cc/G3BP-2FJB)

United States Census Bureau (2019) 2019 Annual business survey, Census.gov. www.census.gov/library/visualizations/2020/comm/business-owners-ages.html (archived at https://perma.cc/93EK-Y2SD)

Conclusion

IPCC (2022) The evidence is clear: The time for action is now. We can halve emissions by 2030. Intergovernmental Panel on Climate Change, p 2. www.ipcc.ch/2022/04/04/ipcc-ar6-wgiii-pressrelease/ (archived at https://perma.cc/8753-9T3M)

Index

CPSIA information can be obtained
at www.ICGtesting.com
Printed in the USA
JSHW041336190323
39109JS00012B/63